PRAISE FOR BRICKYARD STORIES 2.0:
A LYNN MA NEIGHBORHOOD BEFORE AND AFTER URBAN RENEWAL

Brickyard Stories 2.0 captures the soul of a once and still close-knit community. It is readable, moving, and a valuable contribution to the broad American story.

- John Ronan, author of *Taking the Train of Singularity South from Midtown*
  former Poet Laureate of Gloucester MA

…a smooth elegant stream of consideration, fact, grit and memory.

- Joe Boyd, singer-songwriter, member Lynn Museum Board of Trustees

Carl Carlsen's *Brickyard Stories 2.0* is the perfect bookend to his *Brickyard Stories: A Neighborhood and its Traditions* [1985] and Kathryn Grover's *The Brickyard: The Life, Death and the Legend of an Urban Neighborhood* [2004]. In his new book, through stories, poetry and a collection of maps and images, Carlsen brings the Brickyard to life again. This book is not only for those who remember this vital and diverse neighborhood, but also for anyone interested in the history of immigration and neighborhoods.

- Ken Turino, Manager of Community Partnerships and Resource Development,
  Historic New England   former Executive Director, Lynn Museum

Brickyard Stories 2.0 traces, largely through oral history, the transition of the once-beloved physical neighborhood to a remembered place, among those who lived here, and then an imagined place, among those who believe its name connotes solidity, cooperation, and inclusion. Carlsen has always had a feel for the lyrical quality of recollection, particularly when it comes to Lynn's Brickyard, and this hybrid history demonstrates that to him and many Brickyarders, as Brickyard poet Vincent Ferrini would say, "Every living thing is a poem."

- Kathryn Grover, author of *The Brickyard: The Life, Death and the Legend of an Urban Neighborhood*

With a nostalgic working-class charm, this book paints an authentic picture of the Brickyard, but it's really an urban historical sketch that anyone in blue-collar America can relate to.

- Kevin Carey, author of *Set in Stone* and *Murder in the Marsh*

Brickyard Stories 2.0 is a captivating story of a "quintessential American melting pot," demolished, but not destroyed in spirit, by urban renewal. Carl Carlsen provides incisive analysis, and, in the great tradition of oral historians, he lets his storytellers speak for themselves to bring this neighborhood to life. *Brickyard Stories 2.0* captures the sadness of bulldozed homes, a lost "network of social relations," and it also shows how the name "Brickyard" has lived on to signify inclusiveness, creativity, and what one storyteller calls, "a work-ethic rooted in an awareness of deprivation."

- John Nelson, author of *Flight Calls: Exploring Massachusetts through Birds*

The wide range of voices demonstrate not only the ways in which human connections form a neighborhood, but also the ways in which a neighborhood—its rituals, institutions, stories and geographic boundaries—informs the character of those who live there. *Brickyard Stories 2.0* is an engrossing read not only for social historians, Lynn residents and students of oral history, but for all of us who have loved and identified with a neighborhood, who can say with Arnold Trachtman, "I could never leave it behind."

- Kathleen Aguero, author of *After That* and *Investigations: The Mystery of the Girl Sleuth*

These days, we often speak of "community," but these pages give a sense of what a real community actually feels like: the eccentric characters, the daily interactions, the prejudice and generosity, the politics and love, the struggle and triumph. The Brickyard neighborhood that Carlsen brings so vividly to life is rich with sculptors, musicians, writers, the devout and the troublesome, ramshackle houses filled with kids, streets filled with music, fisticuffs, flirting, men keeping bear cubs as pets and mothers whacking neighbors with a broom. I truly enjoyed this book and recommend it enthusiastically to anyone with an interest in the human condition—that strange elaborate, multi-faceted, infuriating and exciting dance we call "life."

- Roland Merullo, author of *Revere Beach Boulevard* and *Breakfast with Buddha*

It's one thing to convey a person: the voice, the stories, the essence. It's another to convey a community: the traditions, the beliefs, the evolution over time. In this deeply satisfying book, Carl Carlsen does both. Using a poet's ear, he unearths the music of citizens' speech, and using a historian's eye, he traces the happenings that define the vibrant, working-class neighborhood of immigrants and the forces that undermine it and turn it into memory. Each voice he preserves is a brick in the edifice of local history Carlsen builds, and his insightful arrangement and commentary, along with Rod Kessler's photos, is the mortar that makes everything take shape, solid and beautiful. Long live the Brickyard!

- J. D. Scrimgeour, author of *Lifting the Turtle* and *Themes for English B*

Brickyard Stories

2.0

Brickyard Stories 2.0

A Lynn MA Neighborhood
Before and After Urban Renewal

For Frank — from dogtown to lynn

Enjoy these Brickyard Stories

Collected, edited and presented by CARL CARLSEN

with photographs by ROD KESSLER

BRICKYARD PRESS   LYNN, MA

Brickyard Stories 2.0: A Lynn MA Neighborhood Before and After Urban Renewal

All stories presented here given orally to Carl Carlsen with permission to reproduce.

Cover image: "Mr. Tillson Makes His Way Through the Brickyard" by Arnold Trachtman, used with permission of his estate.

Photographs by Rod Kessler

Book design and cover design by M.P. Carver

Library of Congress Control Number: 2021903810

Brickyard Press   Lynn, MA
First Edition: 2021
ISBN: 978-0-578-86513-3

1 2 3 4 / 24 23 22 21

"We are Brickyarders all."

—Guy "Chick" Gecoya, author of
The Brickyard Story: Remembrances of Times Past

Brickyard Stories 2.0
A Lynn MA Neighborhood Before and After Urban Renewal

AS YOU BEGIN

PART 1:   THE OLD BRICKYARD   *BEFORE URBAN RENEWAL*

PART 2: THE NEW BRICKYARD *AFTER URBAN RENEWAL*

MORE ABOUT THE BRICKYARD

A SEPTEMBER 8TH 2020 PHOTO SAFARI
THROUGH THE BRICKYARD CORRIDOR

As You Begin

AN INTRODUCTION TO BRICKYARD
STORIES 2.0

1

In the early 1980s, when I started teaching at North Shore Community College's temporary campus in Lynn, MA, people told me about a nearby neighborhood called the Brickyard. I learned many prominent people grew up there, including the two state legislators from Lynn who would enable the college to construct its permanent Lynn building on the site of the Great Lynn Fire of 1981. The more I heard, the more intrigued I became, and I soon embarked on a college-supported oral history project to capture what I believed to be the magic of a neighborhood that had been wiped out by urban renewal. I was inspired by *Voices of a Generation: Growing up in Lynn during the decline of the Shoe Industry*, a booklet of oral histories created by students in NSCC's Upward Bound program.

In 1985, to accompany the opening of North Shore Community College's permanent campus in Lynn, the college published *Brickyard Stories: A Neighborhood and its Traditions*, my collection of poetry and prose drawn from interviews with former residents of the Brickyard. The Brickyard in its heyday was a quintessential American melting pot, multiethnic, multiracial, blue-collar working-class, and within its roughly half a square mile area, successive waves of immigrants gained a foothold on these shores, first mostly Irish, then mostly Italians and Jews.

The Brickyard was transformed by the urban renewal movement of the 1950s and 1960s. A large swath of residential housing was demolished, and in its stead rose apartment towers and garden apartments as well as a new vocational high school. Many of the people I interviewed for that first book had been displaced by urban renewal and were sorry for the passing of a way of life focused on the neighborhood.

2

After the publication of *Brickyard Stories*, I continued to interview Brickyarders, and a community of interest in the Brickyard continued through the 1990s, culminating in the Lynn Museum's sponsorship of historian Kathryn Grover's *The Brickyard: The Life, Death, and the Legend of an Urban Neighborhood*. This is an oversized book, a picture-filled, more scholarly treatment of the neighborhood, still reliant on interviews with Brickyarders, both hers, done in 1999 and 2000, and mine, done in 1982. Grover's book was published in 2004, and in the years since, interest in the Brickyard has waned.

One obvious reason for that is the aging of the Brickyarders who lived there during urban renewal, something that happened over fifty years ago. Fewer and fewer people keep memories of that era and that place alive. The second reason is that for younger people, people who have come to the neighborhood in the decades following urban renewal, the neighborhood is a completely different place. For them, the name Brickyard doesn't have the same resonance, doesn't evoke the "old" neighborhood described by Brickyarders who identify themselves as such.

The newer people in the neighborhood may not think of themselves as Brickyarders and many may be only vaguely aware of the name Brickyard as applied to their neighborhood. And although the legends of the Brickyard may be in diminished circulation and what could be considered the actual neighborhood of the Brickyard in 2020 has shrunken boundaries, the concept of the Brickyard lives on, serving as a brand, an inspiration for creative entrepreneurs. Examples include Brickyard VFX, Brickyard Village and the Brickyard Collaborative. As a brand, the Brickyard represents, among other things, tolerance, self-sufficiency and the capacity to overcome obstacles as well as to help others. There's something classically American about that, and for that reason, the Brickyard, and by extension, Brickyard stories, will always remain relevant.

3

Brickyard Stories 2.0, my second collection of Brickyard stories, is about the connections people have to the Brickyard neighborhood and the city of Lynn. I've tried to capture something essential about each speaker in each story, to select stories that show what lies at the heart of the neighborhood and to represent the diversity of the neighborhood. I didn't find the people I interviewed in any scientifically randomized way. I usually met them by referral or by chance. So, what's here are the stories I've collected from the people I interviewed, and I hope they show the scope and breadth of the neighborhood over time.

I collected these Brickyard stories told by residents, former residents and people connected to Lynn's Brickyard neighborhood from interviews I tape recorded with them between 1982 and 2019. I also used an interview done by Kathryn Grover in 2000, so in all, there are forty Brickyard storytellers gathered here. Seven of the speakers were interviewed in 1982 for the first collection of Brickyard stories and their voices tell new and different stories in *Brickyard Stories 2.0*. I did eight interviews in 1986, following the publication of the first book, and I did twelve more interviews between 1994 and 2007, mostly with students in my writing classes at NSCC. In the last group are twelve people I interviewed in 2019. In all, forty speakers recorded over 37 years, enough to plot the story of the neighborhood through the 20th century and into the first two decades of the 21st.

The Brickyard stories presented here are the best stories extracted from interviews that lasted between forty minutes and two hours. These stories are not exact verbatim transcriptions, but I have aimed to stay true to the individual voices of the speakers. I've intervened to change words and wording for clarity and compression, and I've retained some errors in word usage. In the service of telling the story, sometimes I've moved things around within a story to improve its momentum, direction and structure. I hope it all works for you, that there's enough variety in these stories and the ways they are told to engage and hold your attention.

While the Brickyard stories in this collection capture the personal lived experiences of the storytellers, there are also many other interesting stories about neighborhood events reported as news. James Newhall's *History of Lynn, vol. 2* [1897] includes a note among the Annals of 1869 describing the installation of a drainage system on Shepard St. that had the unintended consequence of drying up a number of wells on the street as well as a small pond on Lynn Common. Newhall writes that, despite the drawbacks, there is "no doubt of the value of such works."

Over the years, I've collected newspaper stories about the Brickyard that have reported both "good news" and "bad news" about the neighborhood. On the negative side of the ledger, in 1986, arrests for drugs were made at a house on Alley St. In 1988, a building on Commercial St. occupied by Cambodian tenants was firebombed. In 1989, mail carriers on Vine St. were given a police escort after complaining of verbal harassment. In 1990, sandblasting on the Shepard St. Commuter Rail bridge released so many harmful particulates into the air that the mayor declared a health emergency, and in 2019, icons were vandalized at St. George Greek Orthodox Church.

On the positive side, in 1982, well-known Brickyard emcee Freddy Ross made a comeback after losing years to alcoholism and it was the subject of columns in both *The Boston Globe* and *The Boston Herald*. In 1997, the pews taken from St. Francis Church after it closed were given to the Inner City Community Church in Knoxville, Tenn., and in 2016, a cat was rescued from the third floor of a burning building on Alley St.

Behind all of these events are the personal lived experiences of the individuals involved. *Brickyard Stories 2.0* contains stories that provide that "up close and personal" view into neighborhood life, in contrast to the more distanced and objective news story. The stories in *Brickyard Stories 2.0* contain, as Ezra Pound once defined poetry, "news that stays news."

As you read through the stories, you'll notice how distinctive each one is and how unique each storyteller's voice is. You'll notice how the details bring the stories alive and you'll notice themes among the stories. Stories about mothers and fathers show the roots of the speakers' families. Urban renewal plays a central role in the Brickyard story. It's often said that everyone in the Brickyard got along because of the close quarters they lived in, and while these stories confirm that, they also show the experience of discrimination in housing and employment among Black Brickyarders as well as tensions between Jews and Gentiles, Irish and Italians. There's also a trace of the reluctance of Black Brickyarders to help Southern Blacks who moved into the neighborhood in the 50s and 60s, as the Brickyard was beginning its decline. Finally, there's a lot of artistic creativity among the Brickyard storytellers. Often a blue-collar working-class neighborhood isn't thought of as fertile ground for nurturing such creativity, but these Brickyard stories more than suggest otherwise.

Many, many stories have been gathered about the old Brickyard, the pre-urban renewal Brickyard that lasted through the first seventy years of the 20th century. *Brickyard Stories 2.0* adds to this trove and expands the scope of stories about the old Brickyard to include stories of lasting attachments, about the way the Brickyard they once lived in remains in storytellers' lives.

Brickyard Stories 2.0 also has stories of the new Brickyard, the post-urban renewal Brickyard of the 1990s and the 21st century. Here are stories about Neptune Towers, the signature development of the Lynnway-Summer Project, as well as more contemporary stories about creative entrepreneurs using the Brickyard name as a brand, as a way to infuse their endeavors with the spirit and vitality of the old Brickyard.

Brickyard Stories 2.0 contains a variety of background materials. Maps depict the history and development of the neighborhood in centuries past. Photographs convey a sense of the neighborhood today. Essays propose the Brickyard has been a crucible for the evolution of urban renewal into neighborhood development and that in 2020, the Brickyard has a literature of its own.

In 2020, the Brickyard is a shrunken neighborhood and an expanding brand.

Brickyard Stories 2.0 describes, explains and brings to life how that happened.

THE BOUNDARIES AND THE NAMING
OF THE BRICKYARD

1

The expanded Brickyard, the pre-urban renewal Brickyard at its most robust, was an area of about half a square mile running south from just below the Lynn Common toward the sea to the Lynnway, a multi-lane highway opened in 1955 as part of Route 1A on the roadway formerly known as Broad St. Before the Lynnway, the Brickyard's southern boundary was defined by the Boston, Revere Beach and Lynn Railroad, commonly called the Narrow Gauge, which was in operation from 1874 until 1940. The Lynnway and the Narrow Gauge follow an almost identical course and together they are emblematic of a cultural shift from railroad to automobile transportation.

The expanded Brickyard was a corridor from the Common to the Lynnway, bounded on the west by Commercial St., at one end of Lynn Common, and on the east by Pleasant St., at the other end of the Common. The commercial spine of the expanded Brickyard was Summer St., which ran diagonally in a southeast direction, north of the Boston & Maine Railroad tracks across the entire corridor from Commercial to Pleasant Streets. It's generally understood that the Brickyard doesn't include South Common St. and some of the area below South Common, but that's a blurry border. Commercial St., the Lynnway or the Narrow Gauge and Pleasant St. are generally thought of as the hard boundaries of the expanded Brickyard, while the northernmost boundary below the Common could be considered a soft boundary.

2

The full-sized tracks of the B&M Railroad, once the Eastern Railroad and now the MBTA Commuter Rail, are a prominent defining feature of the neighborhood that travel across it roughly three blocks north of the Lynnway, between Commercial and Pleasant Streets. The Eastern Railroad began service to Lynn in 1838, then leased its track to the B&M in 1884 before selling it outright in 1900. The process by which the MBTA Commuter Rail took control of the line from the B&M began in 1965 and was completed in 1973, coincidentally the peak years of Brickyard urban renewal.

Both historian Kathryn Grover and I think of the entire area between the Lynnway or the Narrow Gauge and the B&M tracks as the original Brickyard. This includes portions therein of Blossom St. and Shepard St., and all of Alley St. and Harbor St. from Commercial to Pleasant Streets.

Unofficial Brickyard historian Guy "Chick" Gecoya writes in his unpublished 1979 manuscript, *The Brickyard Story: Remembrances of Times Past*, that the Brickyard was first used as the name for a four-block area between the tracks, on Alley St. and Harbor St. from Pleasant St. to Blossom St. A 1905 map of what Gecoya called the "real" Brickyard was published in a 1998 *Lynn Item* article on the Brickyard and a detailed hand-drawn map of the same area done by Gecoya himself is included in Grover's 2004 book, *The Brickyard: The Life, Death and Legend of an Urban*

Neighborhood. So, as I like to think of it, there's an original Brickyard, an expanded Brickyard and even a real Brickyard, and the boundaries of these designations speak to the 20th century growth of the neighborhood within its corridor before urban renewal.

3

According to Chick Gecoya, the name Brickyard as we think of it today was first used by workmen at Shea & Donnelly's stone yard on Harbor St. While doing the stonework on the Lynn Public Library across from Lynn Common, if they wanted a beer after work, they would say, "Let's go to the Brickyard." This meant Lennon's bar, on the south side of the B&M tracks, close to the stone yard, and not another bar, Nicholson's, which was also on Blossom St., but on the library's side, north of the tracks. Maybe too Brickyard was code for beer, a way to avoid mentioning drinking while on the job for a company whose bosses might not approve.

So, while there may have been other commercial concerns dealing in either stone or brick in the neighborhood during the 1800s, this is the first story told about how the Brickyard got its name. However true or not it may be, it's a kind of creation myth, and it's interesting that it's tied to the construction of the Lynn Public Library, a city institution that opened its impressive new building at the turn of the 20th century. And, that the stone yard workers were likely Italian and the owners Irish reflects the successive waves of European immigrants coming to the Brickyard and enhances the historical significance of the story.

Worth noting in this discussion is that Jim Steadman, in his October 2, 1972 *Lynn Item* article, "The Brickyard—A Changed Neighborhood," writes that the neighborhood, "picked up the tag 'Brickyard' in the late 1880s from the Newhall Brick Yard located there." Another record indicates a Kelly's Brick Yard in the area from 1837 to 1858. Kathryn Grover reports that a brickyard owned by the Alley family started in 1832 near Pleasant St. and "stayed in business for about a quarter century." However, Alonzo Lewis and James R. Newhall in their *History of Lynn* [1865] call this enterprise a grist mill.

The derivation of the Brickyard name for the neighborhood is hard to determine with any certainty. What is clear though is that Chick Gecoya's story of how the neighborhood came to be called the Brickyard is the most well-developed of all the explanations, and perhaps because of that, it's the most entertaining, if not the most convincing.

4

The Brickyard has a life and a life story. It's an organism; it expands and contracts. From Chick Gecoya's creation myth that locates the real Brickyard within a four-block area, the neighborhood grows all the way down Alley and Harbor Streets between the B&M and Narrow Gauge tracks, from Pleasant St. to Commercial St., into the original Brickyard. Mostly Irish in the 19th century, many Italians had settled in the Brickyard by 1900. Then, as more immigrants to Lynn come to the Brickyard in the years before and after World War I, the neighborhood expands in people's minds, spreading north above the B&M tracks up the corridor between Commercial and Pleasant Streets to somewhere short of South Common St. and the Lynn Common.

This pattern of growth is borne out by looking at Sanborn insurance maps of the Brickyard. These maps show individual houses and buildings and indicate that on Alley St., between 1905 and 1924, no new residential structures were added. Meanwhile just above the B&M tracks, on Laconia Court, later renamed Summer Circle, a block-long street parallel to and between Blossom St. and Shepard St., the number of residential structures swells by one third between 1905 and 1924. It's reasonable then to assume that over time, as the population increases, the boundaries of the original Brickyard grow into what can be called the expanded Brickyard.

After urban renewal, the heyday of the expanded Brickyard is over. The Brickyard contracts. North of the B&M tracks, much of the land is taken up by a vocational high school and a number of affordable housing towers and garden apartments. Summer St. is no longer a magnet for shoppers. Below the B&M tracks, in the original Brickyard, more of the land is being used commercially and less is used residentially.

5

Today, as in the past, the boundaries of the Brickyard are open to discussion. I'm inclined to respect and acknowledge the boundaries of Chick Gecoya's real Brickyard, the original Brickyard and the expanded Brickyard, to observe the Lynnway and the B&M and Narrow Gauge railroad tracks as distinctive markers, and to consider the "real" Brickyard today as a smaller area within the original Brickyard which preserves the traditions of the old neighborhood. This Brickyard is once again south of the B&M (now the MBTA Commuter Rail) tracks, on Alley St. and the shortened Harbor St. It abuts the real Brickyard of yesteryear, but runs west from Blossom St., not east, and ends at a point on Alley St. halfway between Shepard St. and Commercial St., where the residential section gives way to the commercial. The southern border, the Lynnway, formerly the Narrow Gauge, hasn't changed.

6

Today, whenever the Brickyard is brought up, hardly anyone is interested in where the name came from, but people always remember streets, families and friends, and occasionally, they will speculate about the boundaries of the neighborhood.

MAPS OF THE BRICKYARD

The history and development of the Brickyard can easily be seen on historical maps of Lynn by paying attention to the Brickyard Corridor, extending south from Lynn Common to the harbor and bounded on the east by Commercial St. and on the west by Pleasant St.

MAP 1   EARLY SETTLEMENT IN LYNN

The "Map of Ancient Lynn Mass. From 1650 to the Division of Public Lands in 1706. Drawn by Wm. T. Oliver from Data furnished by Ina T. Moulton & others, Lynn, 1892." shows only one street, Petticoat Lane, extending south from Lynn Common in the area thought of today as the expanded Brickyard. This map indicates The First Congregational Church, Lynn's first church, was located on this street and founded in 1632.

Petticoat Lane was renamed Shepard St. after the Rev. Jeremiah Shepard, who served as the church's minister from 1680 until his death in 1720. A lengthy biography of Shepard in *History of Lynn* by Alonzo Lewis and James R. Newhall [1865] remembers him as a man of "spotless purity of character" to whom "no one can annex an anecdote of mirth." "Mr. Shepard's views of human nature… were of the darkest kind… and these opinions unfortunately led him to regard the greater part of the Christian world as out of the way of salvation, and to look upon the crushed remnant of the red men as little better than the wild beasts of the forest."

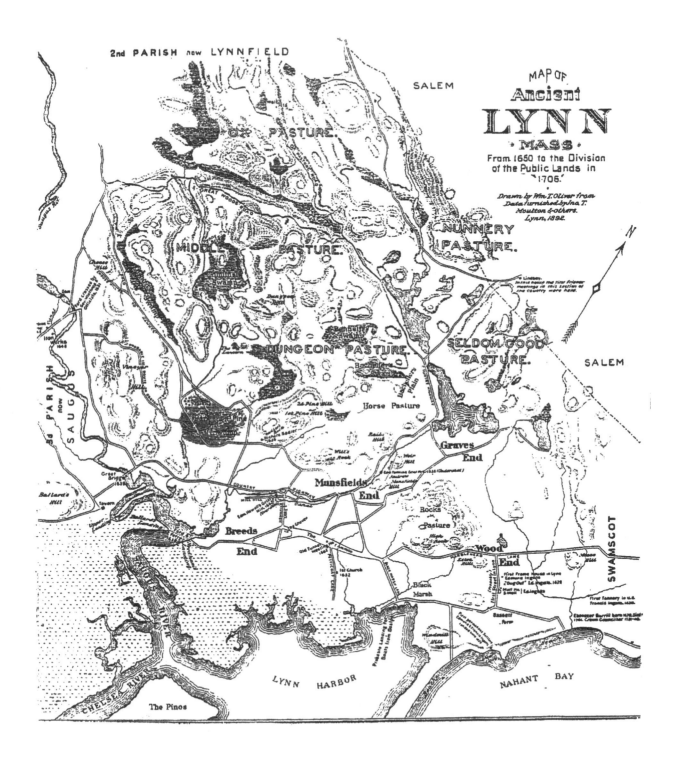

MAP 2   THE TOWN OF LYNN   1829

The corridor of what will become the expanded Brickyard is clearly delineated by Commercial St. and Pleasant St. on "The First Map of Lynn and Saugus, surveyed, drawn and published by Alonzo Lewis (Author of the *History of Lynn*) in 1829. Republished by John L. Robinson, February, 1872." Petticoat Lane is now Shepard St. and the First Congregational Church sits near its intersection with Summer St., which now runs between Commercial and Pleasant Streets parallel to the Common. Vine St. connects the Common to Summer St., and the four Brickyard residents named on the map next to where it shows their houses are all noted Lynn citizens identified in Lewis' *History*. South of Summer St., three streets—Commercial, Shepard, and Pleasant—reach toward the water and a large wetland is visible.

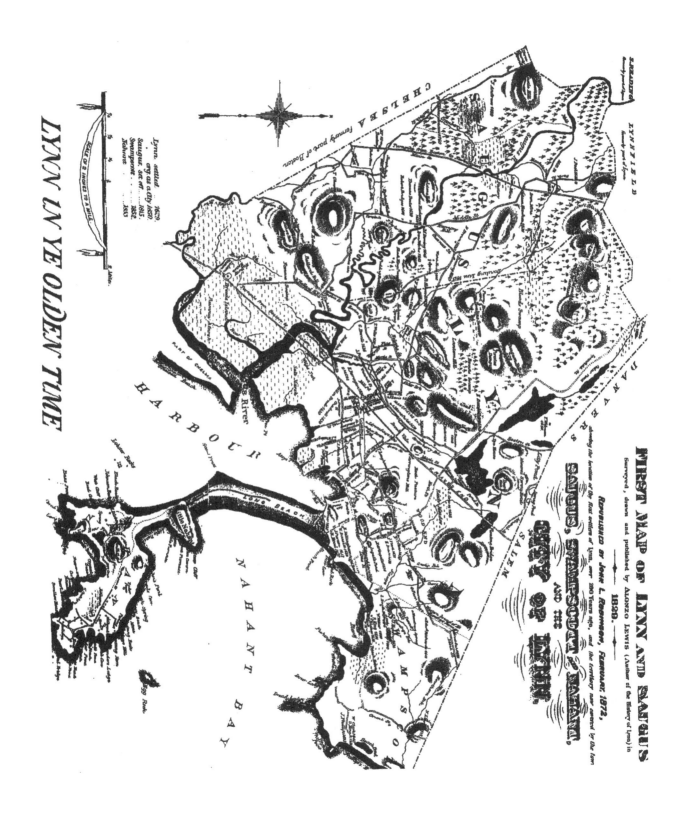

MAP 3   THE CITY OF LYNN   1851

Lynn officially became a town in 1829 and was incorporated as a city in 1850. According to Alonzo Lewis, Lynn's population was 6,138 in 1830 and 14,257 in 1850. This marvelously detailed 1851 map of the Brickyard shows the Brickyard Corridor during Lynn's early days as a city. The map shows the tracks of the Eastern Railroad, which began service between Boston and Salem in 1838. Between the tracks and the Common, there are many more streets, and the area between Summer St. and the Common is much more densely populated than the area between Summer St. and the tracks. Below the tracks, a whisper of development on Pleasant St. Court portends what is to become Alley St., and what will become Harbor St. is called Harvard St. Above the tracks live mainly Yankees and below the tracks, the Alley family, from Ireland, owns property.

MAP 4   THE BRICKYARD   1877

The population of Lynn doubled again between 1850 and 1870 and by 1880, it reached 38,274. The wonderfully evocative 1877 map of the Brickyard shows the addition to the neighborhood of the Narrow Gauge Railroad, which began operating in 1874. The area of the original Brickyard, between the tracks of the Narrow Gauge and the Eastern railroads, has grown substantially. Lynn Gas & Light Co., chartered in 1853, is plainly visible and was an important employer of the Brickyard Irish. The increase in the development of the area between the Eastern tracks and the Common is also evident and is especially dramatic between Summer St. and those tracks.

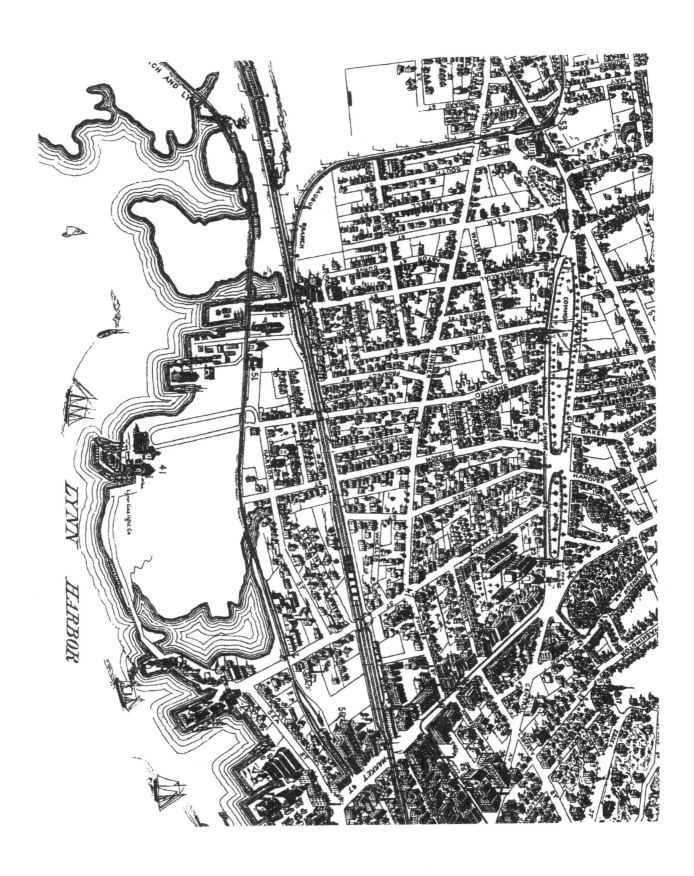

MAP 5 THE BRICKYARD AND SURROUNDING AREA 1894

By 1890, Lynn's population was 55,727, and in 1900, it reached 68,513, nearly double what it was in 1880. This 1894 map of the Brickyard expresses that growth primarily in the original Brickyard between the tracks of the Narrow Gauge Railroad and what is now the Boston & Maine Railroad. (The B&M purchased the Eastern Railroad in 1890). On this map, Pleasant St. Ct. connects with Alley St. at Blossom St., and Alley St. now extends all the way to Commercial St. The major thoroughfares of the original Brickyard are in place. Development also continues in what will become the expanded Brickyard. On Shepard St., between the B&M tracks and Summer St., four small terraces or courts appear, dead ends cut into the block from the street. Above Summer St., these same additions appear on Blossom St., Church St. and Pleasant St.

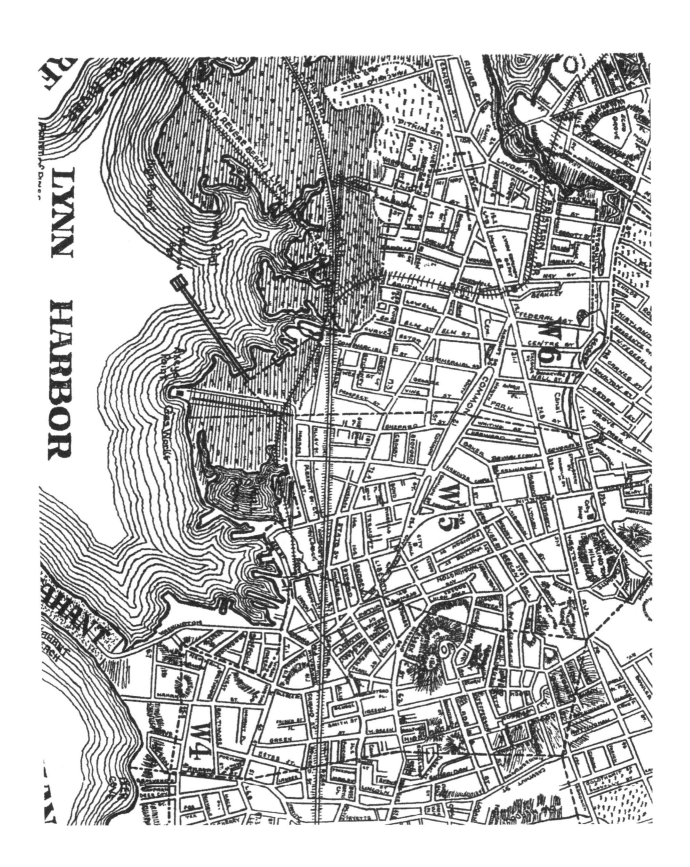

MAP 6   THE BRICKYARD   1927

The 1927 map of the Brickyard represents the expanded neighborhood at its most robust. The wetland below the Narrow Gauge has been filled in; Lynn Gas & Electric Co. and the city stables are prominent occupants of the area. Immigration from Europe peaked, and the newest wave, the Italians, established themselves in the Brickyard. Lynn's population in 1920 was 99,128, a jump of a third since 1900, but because of restrictions placed on immigration, by 1930, that growth rate slowed almost to a standstill.

The city's population that year was 102,320. Since there was a fixed amount of land in the Brickyard, the neighborhood accommodated new residents by creating more small dead-end streets. The burgeoning number of these is evident merely by glancing at the 1927 map. A closer look above the B&M tracks shows Wheeler St. now connects Blossom St. and Pleasant St. Also of interest is Rockmere Terrace, extending in from Commercial St. just below the Common. Row housing was built here in 1900, and these homes are still there today and are known as Rockmere Gardens.

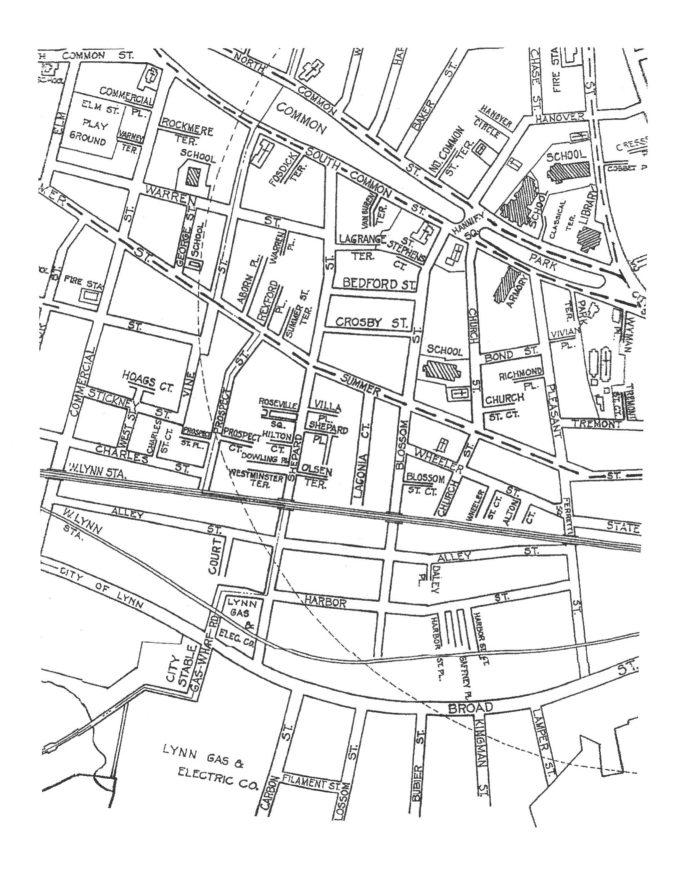

MAP 7   THE BRICKYARD AND SURROUNDING AREA   1957

The 1957 Brickyard map shows the neighborhood before urban renewal. Aside from a few minor changes among the small dead-end streets—the terraces, places and courts—the street plan is unchanged from 1927. The city's population also has remained stable in this period. In 1940, it was 98, 123, in 1950 it was 99, 738, and in 1960 it was 94,478.

One major change occurred on the southern boundary of the original Brickyard. The Narrow Gauge is no longer there, having discontinued service in 1940. And what was Broad St. is now the Lynnway, a modern highway opened in 1955. Finally, the street parallel to and between Shepard St. and Blossom St. running from Summer St. down to the B&M tracks is now called Summer Circle. On the 1877 map, it's Washington Court, and on the 1927 map, it's Laconia Court. The 1957 map reflects the coming dominance of the automobile as well as perhaps, in naming a street Summer Circle, optimism that an old-world pastoral idealism can be preserved.

MAP 8   THE BRICKYARD   1976

The 1976 City Engineer's map of the expanded Brickyard shows the neighborhood after urban renewal. The change in the way the neighborhood looks on a map is mirrored by a significant drop in the city's population. From 90,294 residents in 1970, the population dropped to 78,471 in 1980, a loss of a quarter since 1950.

The 1976 map shows that Harbor St. between Pleasant St. and Blossom St. is gone and so are all but one of the streets between the MBTA Commuter Rail tracks and Summer St. and Neptune Blvd., west of Blossom St. This land was cleared to make way for Lynn Tech and Neptune Towers. Doing so created two Shepard Streets, one between the Common and Neptune Blvd, and the other between the Lynnway and the Commuter Rail, with Lynn Tech in the middle.

Also notable is that Summer St. no longer runs all the way across the Brickyard Corridor. Its east end now branches off from Neptune Blvd. near Shepard St. From there east to Blossom St., the boulevard widens impressively. That thoroughfare merges with Tremont St. one block farther east of Blossom St. near Church St.

Senior and affordable housing developments occupy the land north of Neptune Blvd./Tremont St. between Shepard and Pleasant Streets and south of the Common. Only the streets north of Summer St., from Shepard St. west to Commercial St., are the same as on the 1957 map. Only this small area of the Brickyard Corridor above the tracks was left alone by urban renewal.

THE BRICKYARD: AFTER URBAN RENEWAL

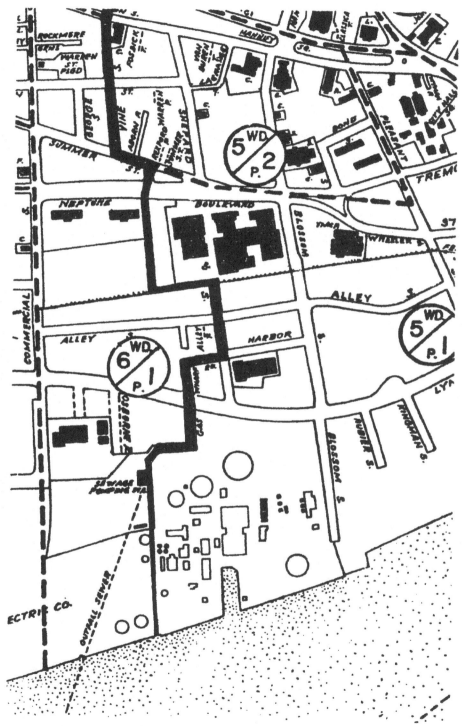

Source: 1976 City Engineer's map

MAP 9 THE BRICKYARD AND SURROUNDING AREA 1999

The 1999 map of the Brickyard in the *Arrow Street Atlas of Greater Boston* shows that the street plan of the neighborhood has remained stable since urban renewal, and interestingly, at a glance, the Brickyard has the same spacious look as it does on the 1976 map. And by the way, in 2000, the population of Lynn was 89,050.

MAP 10   CHICK GECOYA'S "REAL" BRICKYARD   1905

This map of what Chick Gecoya called the "real" Brickyard was published in *The Lynn Item* on November 17, 1998, to accompany an article entitled, " 'The Brickyard' was a great place to grow up." This map details the area in which Gecoya sets his story of how the Brickyard got its name. Lennon's Bar and Shea & Donnelly's Stone Yard are easy to spot.

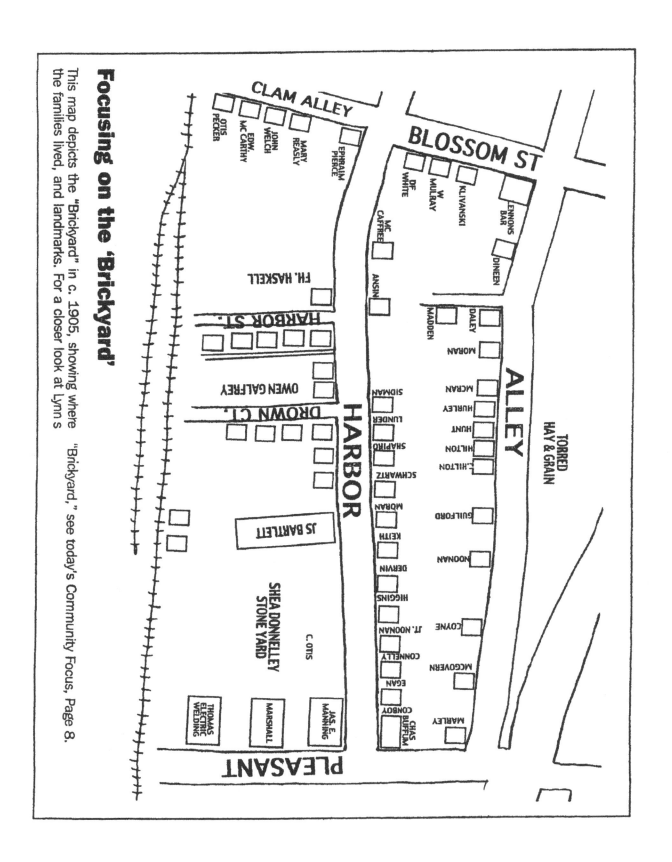

Focusing on the 'Brickyard'

This map depicts the "Brickyard" in c. 1905, showing where the families lived, and landmarks. For a closer look at Lynn's "Brickyard," see today's Community Focus, Page 8.

MAP 11   THE LYNNWAY-SUMMER
URBAN RENEWAL AREA

This last map shows the area of the Brickyard designated for urban renewal. Taken from the *Review of Certain Aspects of the Urban Renewal Program in Lynn, Massachusetts* [1973] prepared by the Comptroller General of the United States, it shows how almost the entire expanded Brickyard was targeted for urban renewal and explains why there is such an empty look to the Brickyard maps of 1976 and 1999.

LYNNWAY-SUMMER
URBAN RENEWAL AREA

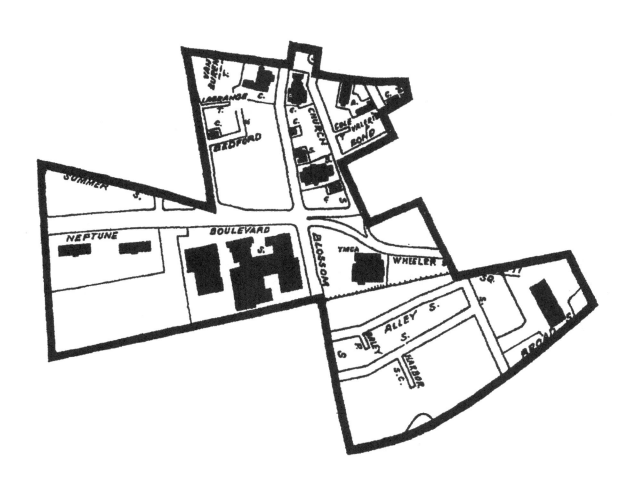

Part 1:
The Old Brickyard
Before Urban Renewal

PROMINENT SECOND-GENERATION OLD-TIMERS OF THE ITALIAN ASCENDANCY

My mother dated Walter Boverini.
He was my gym teacher at Lynn English.
His answer to everything was, "Put ice on it."

My mother would vote for anybody
with a vowel at the end of their name.
She voted the Italian bloc:
Marino, Caggiano, DiVirglio.

If your name ended with a vowel,
you got my mother's vote.
It didn't matter what you stood for.

—Ralph Tufo

1

As an immigrant neighborhood, the Brickyard reflected the major trends in immigration to America in the 19th and 20th centuries. Through most of the 19th century, the Irish were dominant in the original Brickyard between the tracks of the Eastern Railroad and the Narrow Gauge Railroad. In the period from 1880 to 1920, Italians and Jews from Eastern Europe were the largest immigrant groups, and they drove the expansion of the Brickyard up the corridor between Commercial St. and Pleasant St. to its northern border just south of Lynn Common.

2

Edward McDonald's memory of "96 and 99 Alley St.," included in *Brickyard Stories*, recounts his Irish predecessors, the Alley family, and their settlement on Alley St. in the 19th century. A 1998 article in *The Lynn Item*, " 'The Brickyard' was a great place to grow up," states that, "In 1900, the Irish predominated in the area and it was through them that 'The Brickyard' tradition was born and fostered." The rise to prominence of the Connery family best illustrates the Irish achievement of commercial and political success in the Brickyard and in Lynn.

The Connery family coal and wood business, located north of the Eastern/B&M Railroad tracks at the intersection of Pleasant St. and Wheeler St., was known as Connery's Corner. William Connery Sr. was elected mayor of Lynn in 1911 and served one term, and his sons, William Jr. and Lawrence, served nine terms in the U.S. Congress between them from 1923–1941. William Jr. co-authored the Wagner Labor Relations Act, a milestone in union bargaining rights enacted in 1937, which, unfortunately, also legalized inequities for Black workers. Curiously, while Kathryn Grover's history celebrates the political achievements of the Connerys as indicative of the ascendance of the Brickyard's Irish residents to local and national prominence, they are for the most part absent in Chick Gecoya's memoir, perhaps because Connery's Corner was not part of the real Brickyard as he thought of it.

Chick Gecoya's conception of the Brickyard places it within the timeframe of the largest wave of Italian immigration to the U.S., and his *The Brickyard Story: Remembrances of Times Past* is an effort to record and add the contributions of Italians to the history and culture of the Brickyard. The establishment of St. Francis Church on Blossom St. in 1925 and the founding of the Italian American Citizens Club on Harbor St. in 1935 illustrate how Italians created their own institutions in the neighborhood. Of the seven mayors of Lynn who grew up in the Brickyard, two of them were Italians elected to that office as the era of urban renewal came to a close. Patsy Caggiano was elected in 1972 and died shortly thereafter. Antonio Marino won the next election and served as mayor from 1972–1973 and from 1976–1985, thus entrenching the Italian ascendancy.

Chick Gecoya's writing places the Italians at the center of the preservation of the Brickyard through memory in the aftermath of urban renewal. Toward that end, he emceed the Brickyard Reunions of 1973 and 1974, he helped co-ordinate the celebration of the Fiftieth Anniversary of

St. Francis Church in 1975 and his memoir of the Brickyard was published serially in *The Lynn Item* in 1979.

3

In his *Remembrances*, Chick Gecoya, born in 1916, refers to his peers as the second generation of Brickyarders, and this seems reasonable given his view that the naming of the Brickyard occurred around 1900. The four speakers in this first section of *Brickyard Stories 2.0* are all members of that second generation as Gecoya called it, and by the time I interviewed them, they could all be considered "old-timers," as Brickyard elders were often called. What follows are stories of the Italian ascendance to prestige and prominence in the Brickyard and these are the tellers of those stories:

Antonio Marino (1921–2013)

I interviewed Lynn's longest-serving mayor in his office in City Hall on May 25, 1982. He was welcoming and congenial, a real "people person." He didn't seem inclined to talk about urban renewal, despite having been active in resisting it as president of Citizens for a Better Lynn. The story of the skill and creativity of his father Emelio's shoemaking fits nicely into the history of shoe manufacturing in Lynn, The Shoe City.

Armand DiFillipo (1924–____)

Interviewed at The 50 Club on May 18, 1982, Army was cordial and hospitable as he recounted the history of The 50 Club and its link to Lennon's bar. After World War II, five Irish gas workers' union members started The 50 Club in the building once occupied by Lennon's bar. DiFillipo took over The 50 Club and, after the original building was lost to urban renewal, he relocated the business further down Blossom St. toward the Lynnway. Today, known as DiFillipo's Brickyard Bar & Grill, it is owned and operated by Armand's son Rocco.

Enzo "Barchy" DeNino (1924–2007)

On June 1, 1982, I interviewed Barchy at E. H. DeNino Scrap Iron and Metals, his place of business at the corner of Blossom St. and Harbor St. After our warm conversation, he took me next door to the Italian American Citizens Club to meet more Brickyarders. Barchy's father Adamo was one of the Club's eight founding members. Throughout his life, Barchy and the Brickyard were synonymous and he was famous for his love of horses (sometimes pronounced by Brickyarders as "hosses").

Walter Boverini (1924–2008)

Interviewed at his home in Salem, MA on June 27, 1996, Senator Boverini was effusive and very helpful. He handed me a handwritten list of biographical information including notes that he "paid for Boys Club dues by setting-up pins in the bowling alley," and that he "paid [his] YMCA membership by working in the coatroom."

First elected to the Massachusetts House of Representatives in 1970, Walter Boverini became a member of the state Senate in 1972. He served as majority leader in the Senate from 1985 until 1994, when he retired from political life. As the Chairman of the Joint Committee on Education, Senator Boverini acted along with House Speaker and fellow Brickyarder Thomas McGee to secure funding for the permanent Lynn campus of North Shore Community College.

Antonio Marino

MY FATHER

1

My father was at the shoemaker's bench at nine.
He was probably just waxing cord.
In those days they called them cord waxers,
take cord and wax it.

They'd start by cleaning benches,
then later they'd have them do the operations,
the different parts of the shoe so that
when he finally reached the age of about sixteen,
he had accomplished the entire trade of making the shoe.

Imagine, he would measure your foot
and he would make the last with tools.
Then he'd mount the shoe,
the leather onto the last,
and he'd completely stitch the shoe by hand,
with all cords, springs in his hand
and in his mouth.

2

Even at home when I was very very young, he'd correct a shoe that was damaged, stitch it by hand. Marvelous the way they used to do it. He knew all the operations. He came to America, Brooklyn, at the age of sixteen because his brother, of course, had been there, in Brooklyn. He was also a shoe worker, my uncle. He said, "Come over. You can make a dollar. You're experienced."

My father came over, got off the boat and he had a tag on him: "Shoemaker." My uncle picked him up and at sixteen years of age, he was hired by George W. Baker Corporation of New York, and the first job he had was stitching by hand, putting on the soles, he used to tell me—all day long. He can remember the old-timers coming around to his bench and saying, "Look at this sixteen-year-old kid. Watch this kid stitch that shoe."

3

They were amazed by him, so of course, he always made a good dollar, he could do anything. But in his career as a shoemaker, he always thought the arch was the weakest part of the foot, where a person suffered the most. So he designed an arch support all made of leather, shaped like a half moon, and this leather piece, they would rubber cement it, soak it overnight in a burlap bag, and in the morning they would come and the leather would be very soft and pliable.

Then they'd carve the half-moon by hand with a knife so that the middle part would be high and the rest would taper off. So in between the sole and your arch, there was about that much leather that had been carved, tapered off, but in the center you have the full height of that arch support and that supported your arch.

4

Don't forget, people walked a great deal in those days. There was no automobiles. A shoe was a very important thing to a man and a woman because everybody walked everywhere and if the shoe didn't fit right, and did not feel good, your feet would hurt. Then they wouldn't buy your shoe. They'd buy other shoes. Remember this is Coward Shoe, still in existence today, high-priced, high-grade shoes.

5

My father was working for Coward Shoe when he created the arch support. But he wasn't that swift you see. They gave him a guaranteed contract, for a guaranteed annual wage, which became his share of the taking, but if he had known, he would have been quite a rich man. He did not patent, and don't forget, even then, patents rights, if you were working for the company at the time you invented it, they still had control of it.

He had worked for Grossman Shoe Company prior to working for Coward Shoe. Grossman's still exists in New York, and they sued Coward for taking my father away from them and for putting in the arch support. You see, Coward wouldn't allow them to use it. Millions of dollars of suits were filed, and my father testified that he had been working for Coward and not Grossman's, and it became a tremendous court case. It was in 1927. Later on, they made arch supports with a steel shank and put leather on top of the steel to reinforce it even further. Now, they make one piece, a shank with a cover, and they just put it right on.

6

My father came to Lynn because the Coward Shoe Company also made shoes in Lynn and they wanted the arch support brought here where they made the women's shoes. They wanted him to come here and do the women's shoes, teach the men how to put the shank in, carve it, put it in its place, and that's what he did.

Living in Lynn was kind of boring for my father. He was a city man. He liked the action of the big city. He liked to watch the games, the operas. On Saturdays, the young men would go see opera in New York. He liked to gamble, play cards, the fastness of the streetcars, the movies, the theaters and all the action of the city. And of course, there were a lot of his childhood friends there, and my mother's friends were there, so they kind of missed them. They used to go back, every so often. About every month or two they'd visit, and then it tapered off to a year, then just faded away.

7

This city was dull for my father,
but it wasn't dull for my mother.
She was glad to be here.
She said it was a good place to raise a family.
They loved the air, as compared to Brooklyn,
and they loved the water.

They had beautiful water in those days;
it was before the lines got corroded,
excellent water.
My mother liked Lynn,
my father not so much.
He liked more action.

Armand DiFillipo

MY FATHER

My father came to Brooklyn from Ciano,
a small town in Italy.
He had relatives in Brooklyn.
There were other relatives in Lynn who said,
"Come up here," 'cause things were good here.

He worked as a laborer for the city
before there was civil service tests
and he worked for Lynn Gas & Electric
before the union.
He kind of got a bad deal in both cases,
but he didn't complain.
He worked hard
and always had a garden.
He always paid his own way
and stayed off welfare.

We lived at 57 Blossom St.
and everybody knew my father
by his grapevine and his moustache.
He had one of those handlebar mustaches
that they had in the old days
that was really big.

THE 50 CLUB

1

The Lennons before Prohibition had the club as a bar. It was one of two bars in the area that was for local people. This was before World War I. They operated it for quite a few years and the place was a landmark for the people who worked on the waterfront. You had coal barges, sand barges, lumber barges coming in, all of which gradually disappeared. But all those people who worked on the wharf used to meet there, and a lot of the people who lived in the area worked down there, so it became a meeting place. They would have free lunch and now you're going back to the time of nickel beers. Lennon's finally went out at Prohibition, never came back, and the owner who died said in his will he never wanted it to be a bar again.

They used it for storage of scrap leather and paint supplies and then finally, about a year after the war, the District 50 IUE from Lynn Gas & Electric came along and they founded the District 50 United Mine Workers and they used that union title to buy a license and it was established as a private club and that's how they got around the will.

The club originally started as a District 50 union club and there were five members who organized it: Walter Kane, Austin Prendergast, Joe Gilroy, Jimmy Ahearn and Larry Sullivan. It was a nice social place to go for people of the Brickyard, and we had a lot of guys come down— politicians like Nipper Clancy, Eddie Wall and a lot of people who were popular in their day. The club was a gathering place and they used to play shuffleboard and I remember the club was one of the first places in the area to have shuffleboard on the table. They had the old whirlybird fans to be the air conditioning. These fans had to be at least one hundred years old. They were the original fans.

It was quite a place and had one of the oldest bars in the state, a mahogany bar, which, when I took over The 50 Club, was still there. But when the business moved after urban renewal, I took the bar, and finally I sold it because I needed money. It was a mahogany bar with oak paneling. You'd never replace a bar like that today. If you did, it would cost ya, because all the wood was mitered and grooved like a parquet floor. The oak paneling was so hard you couldn't drive nails through it. We maintained it as long as we could and finally I needed money and I sold it. It was a beautiful bar. I wish I had it today to tell you the truth. It finally ended up in a bar in Brockton that they wanted to look old-fashioned.

2

When I came out of the service, I worked for a die shop and when The 50 Club came up for sale, I bought it. After their era, the place kind of went downhill, and I took it over in 1969. I grew up in the neighborhood, I was born on Blossom St., and even as a kid, I knew most of the old-timers. By this I mean guys that were older than me, that were prominent people in the area. I figured I could make a go of it. I did. I made it possible. I raised a family with six children.

We continued to do the things that they did. We had block dances every Fourth of July just for the kids. It was always a nice gathering of people from all over the city who came out of the Brickyard who would always come down that night, before the Fourth of July or on the Fourth, depending on when we held the dance. It was down the club. We would block the Alley St. end of it off and we always got a good crowd. Near the end of urban renewal, houses started disappearing and it was hard to get the people back together, so we discontinued the dances.

We had an organization at the time, like a club, the Connery Civic Association. Before the rink came in, there was a playground here and we dedicated a plaque to the Connery Association at the Connery Playground. The plaque's not there now because when the skating rink came in, the land was sold. The plaque was dedicated to the residents of the Brickyard and the kids who played at the Connery Playground. The plaque has disappeared someplace, I don't know where.

I ran the block dances until a year or two before the club was taken down. I took over the club in 1969 and it was on the corner of Blossom and Alley and urban renewal took the club in 1973. It took me a couple of years to get it together, financially it was hard, but my new place opened up here about four years ago in 1979.

WHAT WE HAD

I lived in the Brickyard
until they tore my house down

My kids were all born
between Blossom St. and Alley St.

I been outta here
for ten eleven years now

It was a much better city then
than it is now
because of what we had

Enzo "Barchy" DeNino

My Father

1

The Brickyard name—they claim they got the name
from Shea & Donnelly, that's all I heard of,
not only from my father, but from other people.

My parents were strict, no such things as allowances,
I never heard of the word. You had to make it on your own.
You had to do something.

2

My father worked hard for Shea & Donnelly. You had to go to eleven o'clock mass at St. Mary's if you worked there. The two partners were ushers there, and if you didn't make that mass, you didn't work Monday. My father always bragged that he had to go to eleven o'clock mass.

My father said they were good people to work for. You had to work a lot of hours and he worked Saturdays, half a day. My father worked there until they moved to Indiana. Then they came back and opened in Somerville, and he worked there until the Depression started and they folded up.

He worked with all limestone. He used to build huge limestone buildings like the Lynn library. He always bragged that Shea & Donnelly were honest people. You had to toe the mark with them. You had to be religious and a straight shooter. Any monkey business, and that was it with them.

Hosses

When we lived on Alley St., actually Alley Terrace, in back of us, on Gas Wharf Road, was a stable where the grain company kept their hosses. That's where I got the love for hosses as a kid. They used to come in about four or five o'clock to put up. The wagon shed was a hundred yards away, and the teamster would throw you on one of the hosses, and the hosses would go by themselves into the barn.

In the 30s, the City Sanitary Department, the Street Department and the Sewer Department all had beautiful hosses. In fact, right now, that stable still stands there right on Gas Wharf Road. Out front it says, "City Stables—1913," the year it was built. We used to play in the hayloft. Some of the stablemen were nice and would let you in to help them a bit. The City abandoned all its hosses in 1936. They sent the hosses to Brighton, over to an auction.

Shea & Donnelly had huge hosses, but I don't remember them as well. They sometimes had four or six hosses to a hitch. They were Belgian hosses, the ton hosses. They weighed a ton. The other hosses were thirteen to fourteen hundred pounds, like the ones I had.

HOT AXLE

Around 1949, when parking meters first came to Lynn,
I happened to be parked at the post office on Willow St.
with my wagon and Tony, my first hoss.
We were parked by one of the new meters
and I still have the picture, which I think
made the front page of the newspaper.

In the heyday of the hoss teams,
everybody was friendlier.
If you were stuck on the road,
you always had a helping hand.
If you get a flat tire today,
fifty cars will go by
and nobody will stop.
In those days,
we used to shine the harness
and grease the axle
every Sunday morning.

If you got a hot axle on the road,
whoever had a wrench and axle grease
would stop.
You see, the steel would expand in the hot weather
and the axle would stick and the wheel wouldn't turn.
You have to take it off and grease it.
If you were on the road, you'd have to unhitch.

Walter Boverini

BRICKYARD STORIES

Oh God, every time
I meet a person that came from the Brickyard,
we start relatin' stories in the past,
and nicknames we used to have,
a quiz on nicknames.
Once we had a Cowboy, we had a Tar Baby,
we had a Pickles, a million Rockys;
there were a lot of Rockys around
in those days.

And we talk about different people
and occasionally we have a Columbus Day... ah,
festivity down in the Brickyard
each and every year
that we... ah, we honor the memory of
the past members of the Italian American Club.

My father was one of them of course,
so we go down and we sit down,
the gang of us, and they come from all over,
and people come from Peabody and Salem,
Saugus, places they've moved to
and ah, we sit down
and we talk about the Brickyard.
We talk about the theaters
and a typical day in the Brickyard
and what we did when we were kids
and I try to tell my kids the same thing:
that we were busy, that we always found
something to do.

FUNNY STORY

We were playing Clemson down in South Carolina
and I'm comin' back in an airplane
with the team of course
and Morris Tobin was Secretary of Labor
he was former governor   he was Secretary of Labor
and he was a BC fan.

He used to come to all the games you know.
So I was sittin' next to him in the plane
and he asked me what I was gonna do
when I get out of college
and I had no idea.
I said, "Geez, I dunno, I'd like to get into the FBI."
Yeah, the FBI at the time was recruiting kids from Catholic colleges.
For some reason they believed they'd be more,
not apt to be sympathetic to the Communist cause you know,
and Communism was the big scare then.

Well, ah, he pursued it you know
and then I got an order from the FBI
and I went for the interview
and I took the test and I took the physical
and I was all set to go to the FBI,
and I was down helping Classical coach football
while I was waiting,
I wasn't getting paid for it, just helping out down there,
and ah, a priest come up,
wanna know if I'd be the head football coach
at St. Mary's High School in Lynn.

And I'm just a kid, just out of college,
geez, head coach, just like sayin'
"Ya wanna coach Notre Dame?" you know.
So I jumped at it.
I said, "The hell with the FBI" you know,
and it changed my life around
and without any regrets you know
'cause I've done everything I've wanted to do
and I've always enjoyed some amount of success.

Urban Renewal

1

I can't see blaming everything on urban renewal
but urban renewal didn't help.
Urban renewal was a disaster.

2

Ah, you know it's like if someone came to me and said,
"Hey, we're going to take your house by eminent domain Walter."
I say, "Why?"
"Well, we're gonna do this. Here's what we're gonna put there."

They had no plan. They just took homes.
And it was a money grab. It really was a money grab.
I believe it, sincerely.
Most people were sittin' on 4% mortgages.
The banks were payin' 6% you know, on your savings.
So I think it was the banks that pushed it, pushed it,
pushed it to get rid of all those 4% mortgages.
And ah… then the people had nothin'.

3

I was gettin' married
so I was moving out of the house anyway.
We had a nice house on Summer St., nice house,
330 Summer St., nice house.
And ah, I was getting married
and I had a brother and sister living there.
We never had a problem with anyone. Never.
We all had new cars in the driveway,
never had a problem with anything.
And ah, my brother and sister, they pushed 'em out,
took the house, moved them out.
And ah, then the house sits there for almost 2½ years.

My sister's payin' rent in Saugus,
my brother payin' rent,
well, he bought a house somewhere else,

and the house is sittin' there for two years, vacant.
And they went in and ripped out, you know,
some of the element went in and ripped out the copper pipes,
everything, the gutters, we had a slate roof on the house.
It used to be an estate, the Plummer estate,
and ah, it was a beautiful home.
We had a railing going up the stairs to the front door,
and I remember an antique dealer comin' up and sayin',
"Geez, would I like to have this railing."
All mahogany. Beautiful railing.

And they leave the house vacant, so I have no,
I have no good things to say about urban renewal.
I don't think it accomplished a darn thing.

4

In fact, you go down Harbor St. right now,
Harbor St. and Alley St. You've been down there?
Those houses look better now than they did then.
They were there when I was born. OK?
Some of those families are still there 'cause we stopped it.
Well I shouldn't say "we" 'cause I wasn't a part of it,
but urban renewal was stopped or they would've taken those houses too.
You take the Fanucci house. You turn down those streets,
you see those homes, you say these homes are better now than they were then.

Even the house I was born in,
I was born right on the corner of Alley St. and Blossom St.
There's a store; it's still there. There's a store—Andy Carbone's store,
    downstairs.
I was born upstairs on the second floor.
The building, it's got all vinyl siding on it now.
It looks better now than it did then.

5

I think it was a group… I wasn't part of it then… I think I was at BC then.
I can't even remember when it was… OK, just after BC, yeah yeah
where the hell was I?… I dunno… I never got involved in it.

See that's another thing… I ran for politics… with no axe to grind.
I had no knowledge of what the hell was going on too much in the city.

I was involved with teaching, coaching, and not payin' that much attention to
    things.

But it was stopped by a group called CBL, Citizens for Better Lynn,
a group that ah, ah, Tony Marino was part of it you know.
And they stopped it at Commercial St. and they stopped it at the bridge.
They stopped at the bridge. In fact the sign's on it.
They stopped it at the bridge so they didn't go any further.

6

Wow, the people themselves
have really expanded the Brickyard now.
I talk to guys, they say
they came from the Brickyard.
They really didn't.
I've always thought the Brickyard,
I defined the Brickyard as from
the Lynn Common down to Broad Street,
down to the ocean you know.

THE EXPANDED BRICKYARD IN ITS HEYDAY: DIVERSE AND DYNAMIC

… Summer night, 1929. Child with his family in the streets of the Jewish district of an industrial city, alive at the corner of Summer and Blossom Streets, delighted by the carnival mobility. He feels his ancient identity and sees:

The day worker sleeping at his doorstep… a band of girls running with linked arms, singing in unison, scandalizing the invalid whose wig and shawl hover over parched geraniums at her window… Reb Wasserman, the harassed Melamed (teacher), furtively buying cigarettes, derided by his students… a frivolous gas flame palpitates in its popcorn cage, is pacified and wheeled into the darkness…

1961, the return: At the corner of Summer and Blossom Streets, in the metal automobile cage, I greet the sweetly socialistic memory of a child's night. An image of that carnival assembly, clarified by nostalgia, and its meaning: Goodness of lives in work, of protection after flight; Goodness of words that enjoin fear to be endurable, of laughter in shadows; Goodness of the loving mediation of pain…

—From a letter sent to me by Arthur Polonsky dated March 28, 1988. To introduce this passage, he writes, "In 1961, in a series of memoirs by scientists, educators and artists, published by a journal of Jewish critical thinking [Judiasm, Fall 1961, vol. 10, no. 4], I wrote of some of the origins of my work and these reflections on moments at one of the boundaries of the Brickyard."

Arthur Polonski (1925–2019) was a Lynn native, though not from the Brickyard, and as an artist and painter, he was one of the leading lights of the Boston Expressionists. During a long and celebrated career, he taught at the School of the Museum of Fine Arts, and at Brandeis and Boston Universities.

The Brickyard as portrayed by Chick Gecoya and Kathryn Grover is at its peak in the years between World War I and World War II. The Brickyard is alive with the strivings of a growing immigrant population. Jobs are found in the neighborhood at Lynn Gas & Electric, Hood's Milk, Shea and Donnelly Stone Yard, Torrence & Vary Granary. Summer St. is the Brickyard's vibrant shopping and commercial spine.

The shoe industry, for which Lynn is known, is thriving at the turn of the century but in decline by the 1930s, replaced as a major employer by General Electric. The Great Depression impacts the Brickyard of course, but economic hardships are remembered less in terms of dollars and cents and more in terms of a spirit of facing and overcoming adversity and of being courageous and creative.

The diversity and dynamism of the expanded Brickyard in its heyday is illustrated in the stories told by these speakers:

Betty Sakaris (1923–_____) and Nick Klangos (1919–1992)

Sister and brother, I interviewed them in Nick's Peabody, MA home during the summer of 1986. Their stories evoke Greek life in the neighborhood, and interestingly, it was Lou Ames' band that marched in their father's New Orleans-style funeral. What's important about Nick's story of starting the first sub shop is the way he tells the story, not whether his was actually the first sub shop ever. The same applies to Antonio Marino's story of his father's invention of the arch support, something Wikipedia attributes to Dr. Scholl.

Vincent Jarvis (1913–1988)

Interviewed on June 9, 1982, Vincent was the first Black elected official in Lynn, serving on the School Committee from 1972 to 1985. He spent his working life at General Electric and devoted himself to community service. He worked with many social service organizations and won many awards for his efforts. For me, the most poignant moment in his storytelling is when he remarks, "I always ached to play for a colored team."

James McNiff (circa 1918–2011)

Interviewed at his home in Salem, MA on May 9, 1986, James explained his lifelong relationship with the house he once lived in at 140 Alley St. The concrete fence he remembers being constructed on Alley St. is still there and is in remarkably good condition for a structure over ninety years old.

Alma Savory (1917–2012)

Many people I talked to about the Brickyard mentioned the name of Alma Savory and I regret never having spoken to her. However, Alma was interviewed by Kathryn Grover in her Summer St. home on April 11, 2000. The beauty shop she owned and operated there was the center of a vital social network among Black women in the Brickyard. Alma's stature in the community was enhanced by her work as an evangelist and assistant pastor of the Bethlehem Temple Pentecostal Church. For Alma, the church was a lifelong passion, and a glimpse into this is given by Doris Harewood's recollection of Alma Savory in her story about Brickyard Pentecostals.

Lou Regosa (circa 1918–_____)

My interview with Lou Regosa took place on August 18, 1994, in the downtown Lynn offices of the North Shore Jewish Historical Society. In 1960, there were over fifty Jewish-owned businesses on Summer St. Sophie Gass, the wife of NSJHS founder Nathan Gass, suggested Lou to me, saying that he could tell me all about the vitality of the stores on Summer St. She was right.

Marguerite (1928–   ) and Gitano "Tony" Puleo (1927–2000)

I interviewed the Puleos at their home in Lynn on June 5, 1986. By that time I had come to know Marguerite as someone keenly interested in all things Brickyard related and enthusiastic about helping me promote *Brickyard Stories.* Her husband Tony, widely known as Tony Signs, was a sign maker who ran his business out of a truck. I admired the home-made folksy style of the wooden lettering on his truck. When he started out after World War II, Tony put up "pirate" signs advertising his business alongside the railroad tracks in the Brickyard.

When we met for the interview, Tony handed me thirteen handwritten Brickyard stories, and they are included here exactly as they were given to me. I didn't correct the grammar or the spelling. These snippets of Brickyard life show the diversity of the neighborhood and the mischief caused by Tony and his friends. And as someone who is Jewish, I'm not sure how I feel about his use of "Jew" as an identifier. But since I remember Tony as very warm, welcoming and talkative, I'm inclined to accept his ways of referring to his neighbors. Jews were part of, yet separate from the neighborhood. Same with Brickyard Blacks. This helps explain why the Italians came to be the ethnic group that embraced and embodied the traditions of the Brickyard more than any other.

Judy Christian (1948–   ) and Chris Maniatis (1949–   )

The two sisters are daughters of the famous Brickyard sculptor Darrell O'Connor (1927–2015). I interviewed them at Chris' home in Lynn on August 12, 2019. Their father was well-known throughout the neighborhood, the city and the surrounding area for his collection of whimsical folk-art-style metal sculptures and other artworks installed in the yard of the family home at 15 Harbor St. The long-time employment of O'Connor, Christian and other family members at C. Bain on Pleasant St. is significant since the building, erected in 1908, was at the time the largest one in the United States specifically constructed to be used for storage. Darrell O'Connor occupies a respected place among the other Brickyard artists in this book: commercial artist Tony Puleo, painter Arnold Trachtman, glass-shard painter Eleanor Fisher, and musicians Lou Ames, James McNiff, Rocco Capano, Jason Taglieri and Ralph Tufo.

Betty Sakaris & Nick Klangos

Betty and Nick Remember the Brickyard

1

[Betty]: I was born on Wheeler St., 59 Wheeler St., and George and Peter were born on Laconia Court. My family came to Peabody first. John and Stacy were born in Peabody.

[Nick]: I was about six months old when they moved to Lynn. My father had a barber shop, and he thought it would be more profitable in Lynn than in Peabody. But with the Depression, he was ending up giving free haircuts. He didn't mind. People couldn't afford to pay, even though it was only fifteen cents to start with. Later on, it became a quarter.

My father came over here from Greece. He was young; he wasn't married. He was a teenager and he worked on the railroad. He worked his way from Peabody all the way across to California, and this is how he picked up the various languages—a little Chinese, a little Italian, a little Russian, a little German. At least he was able to communicate—he had to, living on the road. And then he came back to Peabody and he sent for my mother. My father came over in 1906, my mother in 1915 or '16, and then he bought a house. We moved to Lynn in 1920.

His barber shop was on Summer St. by Pleasant St., right on the corner there with St. Mary's. Later on he opened up a shop on the block with Bond St. and Pleasant. He had a few barber shops; he kept on progressing.

[Betty]: Pa went to work for the WPA to earn some money, even though he had the barber shop. They put him over the Pine Grove Cemetery to dig and he fell down the hole into a grave and come home shivering. He never went back again; he got Nick to take his place.

2

[Nick]: There were seven kids altogether, two girls and five boys. Three of us boys slept in one bed. Five boys in one room and the girls had one bed too.

[Betty]: The girls were separate; the Greeks watched their girls. We couldn't date or anything. We just had a lot of fun playing with one another. The girls thought about sports; boys came later. You couldn't date. It was more or less a known thing without anything being said.

[Nick]: The Greeks would fix you up for marriage. The boys would look out for the girls. They were raised to have respect for girls.

[Betty]: It was a long walk to junior high school and I never had to be afraid of boys bothering me, mainly because my brothers would say, "Hey! Hands off!" And because I had five brothers, my sister and I were quite popular with the girls. I used to think they liked me, but later on I found out it was because we had the brothers. So we were OK with the boys and OK with the girls.

3

[Nick]: The Greek Church [St. George Greek Orthodox Church] was on the block with Church St. and Blossom St., where I used to live. It was the only Greek church in Lynn. The Greeks lived on Pleasant St., Bond St., Wheeler St., Blossom St., Shepard St. Within the Brickyard there were maybe two hundred Greek families.

[Betty]: When school let out, Greek school would start. It would start 3:30, 4 o'clock and would last an hour and a half, two hours. We'd go three times a week and then we would come home. They taught you about the history of Greece and how to read and write Greek. I can read and write Greek. It helped me a lot when I took a trip to Greece in 1980.

[Nick]: She went a lot. I rebelled. I skipped Greek school. At home, they would punish me, put me downstairs, lock me downstairs to punish me.

[Betty]: He wouldn't let his father give him a haircut and his hair was long, and I remember the Greek school teacher chasing him all around the room with a scissors to cut his hair. Wasn't that a disgrace? His father's a barber and the teacher has to chase him around.

[Nick]: I rebelled because I thought Greek school was hindering my learning English. I thought English was the thing to know to get ahead. And I had a teacher in second grade, Miss Armand. In first grade I had a lot of trouble, and then I had this teacher who was helping me learn English and I thought the Greek would bother me, which it did. She took a liking to me; she used to give me a bottle of milk, a graham cracker once in a while. She was very good. She was a wonderful woman. And I was in the fifth grade when she passed away. I was sad because she spent a lot of time with me.

4

[Betty]: Eastertime we always had a nice roast lamb. And Easter was baklava and sometimes moussaka. And what was nice was at night when we had Easter, we would go to church, and Saturday evening late, after midnight, we would walk home with a candle, and it was lit, and we would try to make it home without having the wind blow it out. And if we did make it, we'd put a cross at the top of the door with the flame, and it would make a little black mark. That was considered a good thing, a peace offering. Then we'd have a feast. We'd stay up late 'til four in the morning. My mother cooked up a storm.

[Nick]: And then they had these red Easter eggs. Hard boiled and colored red. And on Easter Sunday people would hit their eggs together and one would say, "Christ has risen," and the other would say, "Truly He has." And if one of the eggs cracked, then that person was out, and it went on and on 'til only one person was left and that one was the winner. The two people crack their eggs together to see who has the strongest egg, and if yours is not, if yours cracks, then you eat the egg.

5

[Betty]: My father was a great singer. And he played the bouzouki and the guitar. He had a beautiful tenor voice. He used to be a cantor in the church and he used to sing opera. Besides popular songs, opera. "When I Get Too Old to Dream" he loved. He was asked to go to New York, but because he had such a big family, he didn't go. He used to sing at USOs and places like that during the war. He'd always sing at home.

[Nick]: He used to line us up, my brothers and I, and you just go, "Aaaahh, Aaaahh." That's how we'd start our singing. We'd get that pitch and go, "Aaaaaaaaaaahhh."

[Betty]: He died in '52. He requested of us before he died that a brass band should play at his funeral. He didn't want us to be sad. They marched to Pleasant St. from the church because Greek custom is to take the body by the house before it's buried. And strange as it seems, now I don't know, my sister said it made the *Believe It or Not* by Ripley. Now I don't know if that's true or what.

[Nick]: At first we were surprised, but then we understood, that with his love of music, he wanted us to rejoice. He didn't want us to be sad—everybody dies. It worked—he got his wish and everybody held up strong.

[Betty]: I didn't hold up strong, I passed out. I took it very hard. I fainted.

Boiled, or Not, at the Jewish Home on Wheeler Street

The Jewish people used to have us light their stoves.
It was their Sabbath and they couldn't do it.

Levine used to be on Blossom St., and he had a store there
and he used to call me in and ask me to light the fire for him.
And then he would give me some candy because he couldn't touch the flame.
It was something about the religion, they couldn't touch fire.

And then on Wheeler St., about in the middle of Wheeler St.,
there was what they called the Jewish Home.
It was where Jewish people used to live and down below,
they used to have the immigrants come over.
Down below they had this great big wire fence
and we used to look in there to see what they were doing.
They'd be stirring, stirring things and we'd be watching.
So everybody thought, "Don't let them catch you or
they'll boil you in there."

So one day a man comes down the stairs and he says to me,
"You're Nicholas, aren't you. Sam Levine told me about you.
You're good at lightin' the fire. Ya wanna light the fire for me?"
I'm standin' there thinkin', "What should I do?"
So in the meantime, he brought me inside to light the fire
and I'm gone for half an hour and all the kids outside
are wondering what happened to me. And one says,
"Nicholas went inside to light the fire," and they went
to tell my mother and everybody got scared
and they called the police down and they come down
and I'm inside eatin' after I lit the fire.

Isn't it amazing how far things will go?
The kids are yelling and screaming.
They thought they were boiling me.
It was good news. I was OK.
Unbelievable.

—Nick Klangos

BETTY KLANGOS USMC

1

As kids, we made our own scooters. Like skateboards—the idea of skateboards—we called them scooters with the ball-bearing wheels from roller skates. That's how I became mechanically inclined. I'd watch everybody and then I used to build them myself. And that's why I was an airplane mechanic in the Marine Corps. You get an idea of how things work and how things turn.

2

The Black people who lived in the neighborhood were good people. We got along well; we played together in the streets. Looking back, I was so ignorant when I joined the Marine Corps.

I was down South and waiting to buy a ticket and I saw the line was shorter on the other side. Not realizing why, I asked myself, "What am I standing in this line for? This line is long. The bus is going to leave before I get my ticket." So I went over there and I went up to the window and I said, "I want to buy a ticket."

The guy looked at me and said, "I can't sell you a ticket. You better go over there." "But there's nobody here," I said, "Why can't I buy a ticket here?" Finally another Marine came over and told me this window is for the Blacks. They have to be serviced here. I couldn't understand that. And when I finally saw them sitting in the back of the bus, that kind of shocked me too. It was so different than up here.

3

I went in the service in 1943. I was in from '43 to '46, two years at Parris Island, South Carolina, and then Quantico, Virginia. I used to work at the Watertown Arsenal— I had a good job— I lived for eight months making a good pay and I end up leaving it.

I was with the first group of women to join the Marines. We went to Hunter's College New York for our group because Camp Lejeune wasn't ready yet, but they had all the drill sergeants come up there and drill us. I felt the Marines were a better group—tougher and a better uniform, and I had a lot of patriotism in me at the time.

I could tear apart a whole Pratt & Whitney engine—2800 horsepower—and put it together again. I was the first one to be sent to Parris Island South Carolina to the airplane hangar as a mechanic, a woman mechanic, and they were all basing it on my behavior whether any other girls were coming, so I had to really show I was good. I didn't have my brothers to look after me; I had to rely on myself.

So the training my mother gave me as far as self-control and being good helped a lot. You can't just go into a base with all men and one girl, you know what I mean. You have to have good morals and a good reputation. I was the only one for several months and then they called in all the others. I felt so proud.

Later on they gave me an SNJ, which was a two-seater, and I used to fly co-pilot when the pilots took us up after we worked on the airplane because they always wanted to make sure that they trusted us that we did a good job.

4

In the Marines, they have their own lingo, and you have to learn the terminology. They don't teach it to you. They probably would have if I had gone over to New River North Carolina, where the girls are now. But I went to Hunter's College and it was mostly Navy. We heard the Navy terms before we heard the Marine terms.

Then all of a sudden when I got to the base and they says to me, the girl says, "Hey we're gonna have a GI party." So I looked at her and I says, "Great." So then I started getting ready. I took my shower for the GI party and I'm putting my makeup on. I'm getting all dressed up and then everybody else is doing work. I said, "What the heck's the matter with these people?"

So finally, you stand at attention and it's a good thing I already had my bed made. Come to find out GI party didn't mean a party with the infantry like I thought it did. It meant inspection. GI meant General Inspection. So it's a good thing I was able to pass.

5

My brother Stacy was killed in the Navy. When Stacy got killed, they gave me a furlough. He died April 24, 1945. Stacy was a great swimmer. He and Rocco Mitchell, who was also from the Brickyard, would swim all the way from the beach to Egg Rock and back.

How he got killed was with the Kamikaze planes at Okinawa. He was on a destroyer. He died saving someone else's life. A Kamikaze plane crashed into the ship, but it hadn't exploded yet and a buddy of his was trapped down below. So he went in and down there and pulled his buddy out. He was carrying him and his buddy was wounded over half his body. And then the plane exploded and Stacy was hit and he died two weeks later. They amputated both his legs. He was a great athlete.

I have his diary. He kept a diary while he was on the destroyer. It was like a log of the goings-on on the destroyer. Somebody else started it, and then he took it over and as you read it, it gets more personal. He died a hero, saving another sailor. It was 520, the USS Isherwood. Up until the day he was killed, he was writing in that diary.

—Betty Sakaris

ATOMIC SUBS ON BLOSSOM STREET

I had the first sub store right at the corner of Blossom St.
A lot of these sub shops that you see around now—
back then—they were non-existent.
I opened that place as a variety store right across from St. Francis Church.

At Champion Lamp, my sister worked there,
and she used to come down and get a sandwich.
And the other girls there said, "Bring us back a sandwich too."
So half a dozen girls gave her the money and she came down.
So I went and got the big French bread and I made a long sandwich. And I cut it.
The reason I used that long bread is that I had the American bread,
but they liked the French and Italian bread.
So I got the long two-footer and I cut it into six-inch pieces.
It was easy to make the whole one thing and cut it.
We called it a submarine because the round bread was shaped like a submarine.
And it went over big.

So my brother John come in the store one day
and he says, "What are you making?"
and I says, "I'm making these long sub sandwiches."
So he says, "Atomic! Call 'em atomic subs."
He made me some signs and he brought 'em in.
And I had hung up there: "Atomic Subs."

And those were the first submarine sandwiches.
And it started to catch on fire and it grew so big
that in the summertime, I took a place on Washington St.
This guy had an empty store there and I said,
"Can I have that store? I'm looking for something for the summer."
"Go 'head," he said, "Take it,"
and he charged me five dollars a week for the rent.
So I opened up a sub-shop stand and I had
quite a few fellas from the Brickyard who were working there for me
making subs and we're selling hundreds of them, puttin' 'em out like crazy.
Those were the first two sub shops that were in the city or anywhere.
We were the only place in the country.
That was about '48, '49, around there.

—Nick Klangos

Vincent Jarvis

MY ROOTS

Back then, most Black people in Lynn had their roots in Nova Scotia. They are very clannish you know. I suppose it's because they've never been tied down. They're not comin' from slavery.

My great grandmother came over on a ship from the islands and we had a picture of her once. She was about six foot tall, a very strong woman with hair way down her back. She had very copper-colored skin and she was either a woman-in-waiting or a servant to some rich white woman. She came over on a ship into St. John's or Digby, someplace, and drifted down around Weymouth.

My great grandfather was only a little short man, quite fair, but you did what he told you and that was it. Somehow they got together. My mother was from Lynn, but my father's family had been in Nova Scotia for several generations. My father and my uncles came to Cambridge first after working in lumber camps in Maine.

BASEBALL

1

I lived at 96 Shepard St., a duplex with four families in it. That house had gas for lights and it had a nice furnace and that was something to have around 1918. Right across the street was Marshall's store. Later on it became the High Hat and different barrooms. He had his stable right across from 96 and that's where we played our baseball because he had a big field out front. For bases we used boulders.

2

On the corner of Summer St. was Stone's bakery. The son of the owner liked baseball and I was always crazy about baseball. No one ever saw me without a glove in my back pocket. The son Ben was older than us and we used to play with him and we were glad to play with someone older. He always used to do the batting, but this was fine with us.

3

So when the policeman came along and caught us in the street playing ball, he told us he was going to arrest us, and I remember this as if it was yesterday: he said to us, "Why don't you bring your father down here Saturday morning, and if you don't, I'll put you in jail."

Boy, everybody was scared of jail, so I told my father. My father was gentle, but he was quite a guy if he got stirred up, but he didn't get stirred up very easy. He agreed with the cop, Mr. Peabody, I remember his name. I don't really think that was the last time we played ball in the street; we didn't really want to walk down to where Connery Park is now to play.

THE CRYING ROOM

In East Lynn was a man named Fentin who ran a mattress place and there was a three-decker there and he later went into the leather business and he used to hire us to put skin up on a wall. It was called tacking. Anyway, Fentin died and the three-decker became empty and at that time it was nothin' for people to move into empty houses.

Anyway, Percival Harmon and Jack Nickerson formed a partnership and went down to the Oxford Club, which is where the welfare office is now, and they got a hold of two pool tables for a price. They brought them back and they put them in this three-decker and they had everybody cleaning out the first floor and on the second floor they put up a boxing ring and that ring was called The Crying Room, and I don't think there was a boxer, black, white, green or gray that had never been up in that ring.

So we had the pool room downstairs and the boxing ring upstairs and the older people decided to have a gambling room on the third floor and we kids, we'd have a whisk broom and whenever we saw the cops, we'd reach up and press this button with the broom, and it would send a signal upstairs, and then we wouldn't hear any noise coming from up there anymore.

THE COLORED GIANTS, THE NON-COMPS AND THE BURRIS ALL-STARS

1

When families moved from Blossom St. and storefronts became vacant, they were taken over and sometimes used for athletic clubs. These clubs had teams that could be called semi-pro teams. Different neighborhoods and parts of the cities would have clubs and name them after streets or give them other names. For instance, at 107 or 108 Blossom, Louis Portnoy had the Blossom A.C.

We had an all-colored football team up in East Lynn called the Colored Giants. We had quite a ball club. We had two or three fighters on our team and they were better fighters sometimes than football players. I was quarterback and captain.

The football team formed when we decided to have our own team, since different players were playing with different teams and I always ached to play with a colored team. We put notices in the paper to find teams to play just like all the other teams did. So we played them all and we beat quite a few of them. The Colored Giants football team played about 1932 and 1933.

2

We also had a baseball team called the Non-Comps, which was the name of a colored baseball team in existence before I was born. Then there was the Burris All-Stars. Up in West Lynn is Burris Square and this square is named after a World War I colored hero. So we took the name and had a baseball team and we played in about three different leagues, and depending on how tough the team was that we were playing, we'd bring different players. And this is how the colored fellows in the area got to know each other.

In those days, a colored fellow didn't get into the big leagues, so they just ended up having jobs. A lot of these players were very good. We played with the Malden Bisons and some of the players went on to the Boston Tigers, but I never made too much money playing with these guys.

James McNiff

JAMES MCNIFF'S BRICKYARD

1

Growing up, my best friend was Ozzie DeNino, Barchy's brother. The DeNino's lived in the last house on Alley St., what used to be Hart's property, a two-family house; they lived on the second floor. There's a vacant lot there now. There used to be three three-deckers and they lived in the back house, right next to me.

2

We were, I would say, probably the most well-to-do people on the street. It didn't matter; nobody was any better than anybody else, but it just so happened that we were, as far as I know. And that was before we were struck by misfortune. We had our own property. We had three houses on the property.

My house at 140 Alley St. stands alone now. There's two vacant lots on each side. Let's say, facing my house from the front, the houses that were on the left were all torn down years ago. The ones on the right, there was a big fire there a couple of years ago and it all burnt down.

3

Next to us on the top floor, what used to be Hart's property, a three-decker, the people on the top floor, their names were, their name was Antonelli, an Italian man, and they used to have a player piano, and on hot summer nights, they used to play that player piano, and most of time, the song that was so popular that they used to play, that song more than any other song was "Happy Days Are Here Again." [laughs] I can hear it now. They all used to sing along with it, three or four girls and at least two boys that I know of.

WHY WE MOVED OUT OF THE BRICKYARD IN 1942

My grandfather moved to the Brickyard because he worked for the Narrow Gauge Railroad. I think he was a fireman. I think, I'm not positive. And my uncle, one of his sons, he, ah, he might have been a fireman, but I do know in later years he was a night watchman. He used to go to work every night, and, as you probably know, that was a nice railroad, but it went bankrupt years ago and he lost his job. When he did, he didn't get a cent. There was no Social Security in those days, and there was no pension, and he had to live on what money he had saved.

We left Alley St. in 1942 because you know why? The place was too big, getting older, and it became neglected, needed repair, painting. We had two different families, at two different times of course, they lived in the second house in back, and everybody was poor, and they couldn't afford to pay the rent, they lived there for nothing. My mother let them live there for nothing,

And I guess she got sick of it, and I was young, and we owed about five years in back taxes, from 1937, two hundred dollars a year, five years, a thousand dollars. I graduated from high school in 1936. And I mentioned to my brother-in-law the other day that way back, maybe 1932, 1933 maybe, my mother was offered $55,000 for that property and that was a hell of a lot of money. That was a lot of money. She did mention it to me, but she had no idea of selling it at that time.

I was young, and my uncle of course lived with us, and it got to a point where he wanted to make a change and spend the remaining years of his life in peace and quiet somewhere where he could have it. So my mother looked to find a place for just us and we left the Brickyard and went to live on Whiting St., north of the Common.

A couple of years ago I drove by, and the house across the street from my house, he fixed the place up and it looks good. The last time I saw 140, it maybe needed to be painted. It's a shame when I think of it. That place, it never should have been let go of, for a lousy thousand dollars. It was pathetic, but at the same time, after what my mother went through, the hospital bills would have been so terrifically high that they probably would no doubt have absorbed the property and the value of it, so she had to sell it.

NO CRACKS

George Casale, he lived at 93 Alley. He had brothers-in-law, cousins, relatives, they came from Italy. They were visiting him. And they built that concrete balustrade fence right out in front of the house. Have you noticed it? I went by and I said, "I can remember that when I was a kid." I used to walk by, and I always noticed it when they were building it, and of course, I noticed after they had built it. And today, when I drove by, I says, "My God! I can remember that fence when they were building it and there isn't even a crack in it!" Everything is intact. Usually winter damages concrete, but there isn't a single crack in that fence after all these years. I didn't know them. I was pretty young. I was only eight, ten.

PULL & TACK, PULL & TACK

My grandfather worked, my uncle worked, my father worked, my father worked hard. He was a, a tacker, a tacker in a leather shop. He worked for A.C. Miles and before that, years ago, L.B. Sutter. And he made over a hundred dollars a week. That was big money way back. A tacker—see what they used to do, they used to tack two skins on each side of a board, four skins on each board, and they had a combination tack and pull. They'd pull the skin and tack, pull and tack. Pull and tack and walk around the board. My father was very fast and he did so well, the fellows who were not too fast, he used to help them do their job to help them make more money.

WHISKEY PETE

One fella, he used to get drunk all the time, they called him Whiskey Pete. I can remember him smashing his fists up against that cement wall on the bridge at Shepard St., where the B&M trains used to go over. He used to bang his fists up against that cement wall. Oh, he used to hit his knuckles and they were all bloody. My God, he used to get drunk and he used to go crazy. And that's what he used to do. And he had a crooked nose, probably broken in a fight. He was a real drunkard, an alcoholic. And I don't know whether it was him or not, but my father saw this fellow walking and he couldn't walk straight. And I said to my father, "What's wrong with him?" And my father said, "Oh, he's got tight shoes on."

MY SAX

1

In those days, money was out of style. There wasn't any work. But I was lucky enough, I had my instrument, and I was only a kid, and I used to make a few extra dollars by playing, you know, my sax at night. I played in the high school orchestra and then later on, when I was older, I don't know if you, do you remember the ah, did anybody ever mention it to you, the ah, Penguin Club over in Nahant.

I played there about three years and it used to be, we used to play seven nights a week. Six nights a week, dining and dancing, and on Sunday nights, no dancing, so they used to put on a complete new different floor show just for that one night. We opened the place up back in 1940.

2

I hadn't played for years, for years, up until four years ago. And I said to myself, "Whadaya gonna do when you retire?" so I picked up my sax and started playing, practicing, and I, ah, never thought that I would, actually, but it seemed that I heard a voice, saying somethin' to me, "Why don' you, why don't you now?"

I went by the church, I just stopped, went in to see one of the priests, and I asked him if I could, if he'd be willing to have me, to let me, and he said, "Of course," and he asked me to see the organist, which I did, and I only intended to play two or three times to get it out of my system, but there it is. I've been playing almost four years now. I play with the organist either during Communion or the offertory. I usually play during the offertory. I play about every three weeks, the four o'clock mass on Saturdays.

3

And it's the greatest thing that ever happened to me, the greatest thing. I try to find an adjective to describe the way I feel and I just can't do it. It's the greatest feeling anyone could ever possess. I play for my wife's father and mother, and I play for my father and mother and my uncle, who was so good to me, and I play for all of the musicians, living and deceased. It means so much for me to do it, the greatest feeling, very, very difficult to describe.

Alma Savory

ALMA SAVORY'S BRICKYARD

1

You know, it's the funniest thing, I never knew until, let's say it's been a few years now, that this is the Brickyard. I didn't know this is the Brickyard. I don't remember hearing that growing up.

2

I was born on 49 Neptune St. on nine-twelve nineteen seventeen. My father was born in Barbados and worked at the GE for 35 years. My mother was from Barbados too.

3

I never thought I would live to be, I call it livin' in jail in your own house. Havin' an alarm. We'd go to bed at night and wake up: "Oh, somebody forgot to lock the door last night." Now you lock the door, you shake it, you put the alarm on.

We've got that big steel door, but years ago, we had an ordinary wooden storm door with a screen. And you know, air condition wasn't heard of then, so upstairs, our bedrooms were upstairs, and we would leave the door open, just a latch now, so the air can go upstairs. You wouldn't dare do it now. I won't even sit on my front porch. I'm leery 'cause there's so much crazy people.

My Business Advantage

They called me Elma, and I could never stand Elma, so I started using Erlene, and when I went away to school, all my friends knew me as Erlene. I went away to New York to beauty school and came back and started the beauty shop.

I opened my shop in 1939. I named it the Premiere 'cause it was my premiere. I used to tell the other hairdressers, "Don't keep up with me." Number one, I never married. I had no children, no husband to worry about. I was still my mother's and father's baby as you'd say. I never had to worry about meals. My mother was there; she was very active. She didn't really take down sick until her early 80s, so I had nothin' to do but work. My business and my church work.

I said to the hairdressers, "You can't do like me," 'cause I used to be friends with a lot of those girls. It took time to build up a business. There was a time I got so tired 'cause it takes time to build up a business. The best way to build up a business is your work. I can maybe count the dollars I spent in advertisements. If you satisfy a customer, they will come back, and if you don't satisfy them, they won't come back.

Mine was the first registered licensed Black beauty shop in Lynn. I retired when I was 63 or 64. The only thing I love better than my work is working in the church. That comes first.

I had two chairs. I rented one out to another girl. My sister worked with me for a while. We had people waitin' for us, waiting for us. We never got through. Never. It stayed busy. I had no problem building up a business. I would say, "You can not do like me," 'cause see, when I got through workin' a ten- or twelve-hour day, and my mother used to get disgusted 'cause I wouldn't stop to eat, and she'd bring the food, you know like, and I'd just have to step out into the kitchen, and sometimes I wouldn't want to stop.

But see whenever I got tired, all I ever did, straighten out my books 'cause I have to deal with Uncle Sam, and sometimes I go right upstairs to my bedroom. I say, "Remember, you got to worry about your husband and supper and school and the children's clothes for school," and I didn't have to do that.

And then when my father retired, it was worse. He cleaned the house. I could even leave my uniform. My mother took care of all that. So I say to them, "Don't try to be like me. I got an advantage. I'm spoiled."

Lou Regosa

LOU REGOSA'S BRICKYARD

In the early 1920s, I never lived in what they called the Brickyard area. I was across the Common and lived on Whiting St., but my early childhood, or a good deal of it, was spent over in the Brickyard area. My father owned three three-deckers, which he had built on Aborn Place, which is off Summer St. between Shepard and Vine St. And on Aborn Place, there was a big lot there, and this was back in 1914 or so, when he built those three three-deckers.

And in those days, Sunday morning was the time you went and collected rents, and I always, when I was perhaps five or six years old, I used to go with my father, and sometimes he let me knock at the door and collect the rent, which if I remember was about five dollars a week. These were heated by furnace, which the tenant heated, but they were two bedrooms, a living room, a dining room, kitchen and a bathroom. And when you look back, you wonder how you could get so much for your five dollars.

Sometime in the mid-20s, he decided he'd go up 25 cents. And don't you think the people complained to me when I came to collect and I told them it's 25 cents more. Hey, it's unbelievable; there are people who drop a quarter these days and they don't bend over to pick it up. Gee, talk about what a quarter meant in those days.

MY FATHER

1

My father came to Lynn in the early 1900s. He came from Poland, which was under Russian rule at the time, and he came through Ellis Island. He stayed in New York, but it wasn't his kind of place, and then he came to Lynn, and I don't know why he picked Lynn.

2

My father was a religious man. My mother kept a Kosher home. On high holidays, we went to an Orthodox synagogue on the corner of Commercial and South Common. Anshei Sfard was a small synagogue. In those days, everything around was Orthodox. It wasn't until the late 1920s that a Conservative came in, which was Temple Beth El, which built a temple up here on what they call Breed St.

Up until then the two prominent synagogues were Anshei Sfard and Ahabat Shalom. And people who came from Russia or so went to Anshei Sfard. They called that the Russische shul, and the other, Ahabat Shalom, on Church St., they called that the Litvische shul, which is people who came from Lithuania and that area. But it's strange, it's hard to tell why people went to which synagogue because my father's brother went to the synagogue on Church St. Now they came from the same area, but that was their choice.

3

When I was seven or eight years old, my father enrolled me in the Lynn Hebrew School, which was located on Blossom St. He was a builder and he and his brother, they had a building company; they called it Regosa Brothers. They started in 1922 and built the Lynn Hebrew School, which was dedicated in 1923.

My father was always involved in the Lynn Hebrew School. He was the builder; he was always on the board of directors. I think he was treasurer for many years. Before it was built, they used space on Church St. at Ahabat Shalom.

4

On the corner of Shepard and Summer Streets, there was a barn there. They might have kept horses, this could have been in the early 1920s, and my father bought that piece of property and he tore down the barn. There was a house in front; I think he kept the house. The barn was in the rear and he tore that down and he built a garage and he leased out the garage and finally the people who leased it bought it. They used to call it Shepard St. Garage.

I used to go over there with my father. The person who ran the garage, and it's strange, but down in the cellar he had a bear cub. I don't know where he got it. And I used to go down to look at the bear. That part I remember. I don't know how long he kept it, but when I went over there, I'd ask him if I could see the bear.

SUMMER STREET: THE SENSORY DELIGHTS

1

Of the many businesses on Summer St., and one of the big food stores, non-Jewish, was J.B. Blood's. Very big in those days. As kids we used to walk into the store just to smell the coffee grinding and the peanuts roasting. Looking around, we never bought anything; we just walked through the store.

2

I look back and I think of the quality of the food. I remember this fish market, and the fish were almost dancing when you came into the store, and they would cut 'em up and sell 'em to ya. We'd be with my father and he'd buy some fresh fish, we loved flounder, and it seemed as though nothing ever tasted so good.

3

And some of these delicatessens, if I recall, a corn beef sandwich, a good corn beef sandwich was around fifteen cents and a cherry drink was another ten cents. And it was a real enjoyable meal.

And oftentimes, you went to one of these delicatessens and they'd say, "Well, the corned beef is still being cooked. It'll be an hour." And you'd come back in the hour and get what they called "a real fresh corn beef sandwich." They cut the meat while you were there. It wasn't always sliced up in a pan for hours and hours.

4

Then there were what they called Kosher live poultries, where you went in and you picked out your chicken and they slaughtered it, done in a Kosher way, and they dressed it and you brought it home and you put it in your oven and I keep saying, "I don't think of anything that tasted so good as a fresh-killed roasted chicken or a duck or a goose." I look back and I say, "Oh, was that good eating!"

In those days, no-one was concerned about fat, and in those days, Jewish people used chicken fat in their cooking. In those days, things that were made with chicken fat had a certain, ah, taste, which in those days, was very appetizing.

5

The fish market, there were several, but the one where we used to go, it was on Blossom St. It was in this, eh, well, I don't know if he was actually a fisherman. His name was Goldstein, but I can picture him. He was a short man, and he had a little space in Shapiro's butcher shop, which evidently, he must have rented, but I can picture him. For some reason he always had on rubber boots. And there were only certain times that you could get the fresh fish. You could come over and he'd say, "Hey, I haven't got any fish today."

6

I don't know why, but you look back and you say, "How come things tasted so good in those days?" And they really did. You talk about a delicatessen, and I mentioned the corned beef, but later on in one of the food markets called Leschner's, which came in in the 1930s and became a very popular market, they also sold delicatessen, but if you ever tasted his rolled beef, you would say, "You talk about the gods with ambrosia or nectar." Oh! Did I love what they called rolled beef. I haven't heard of rolled beef any more; I don't know if you could get such a thing. I just remember how tasty it was, especially when it was sliced, just sliced, just made.

7

And of course, one of the other things down on Summer St. was the bakeries. This family, Freedman, F-r-e-e-d-m-a-n, was sometime in the 30s, I think they came from New York, that's how they called it The New York Model Bakery, and they opened a bakery shop on the corner of Summer and Blossom St., and all the children evidently worked in the bakery, and they seemed to be the busiest bakery there.

In fact, on a Saturday, I can remember like six girls waiting, and in those days, before they got the know-how, it used to be, "Hey!" the one that shouted the loudest "I'm here!" was the one they waited on.

Then finally somebody got smart and says, "Hey, let's give 'em out, let's give out numbers." And then they started out numbers, because, hey, if you weren't aggressive, you could be there all morning, 'cause everybody there yells, "Hey! I've been here. I'm here."

But you talk about the breads and the rolls and the pastry. They survived until the urban redevelopment and that was the end of them and the end of you might say the whole Summer St. area.

SUMMER STREET: THE SECRET SAUCE

I can't believe the vitality the area had. There were stores there that I say would be existing today if they had left them alone and provided some areas for parking.

These people knew how to run a business. They made deliveries; they had personal connections with their customers. And you could tell that they were doing well. We used to judge by whether they bought a new home or they fixed up their home, or if they got a new car, you'd say, "Hey, they're doing well in that butcher shop." You knew where they lived and you knew their cars.

And it's strange, back in the 30s, Stop & Shop, they had a store on Summer St. between Shepard and Blossom, and their name was Rabinowitz, and then they changed it to Raab. And I remember we used to buy in Rabinowitz and that because the manager, Mr. Brinner, he was a very personable man. In these stores, you went there because oftentimes, you liked the person.

And you talk about courses on salesmanship and management. These people had it. They didn't need to go to any management school. They didn't need to get an MBA. It's unbelievable if you saw how these people operated. They had it. The only thing is, when the kids went off to college and came back and wanted to change the whole world, in some cases, that was the end of the business.

OLD MAN MISCOLA, OLD MAN MOHAWK AND THERESA THE BALLOON LADY

Old Man Miscola

We used to get mushrooms too. You always go after a rainstorm. But you had to know the right one to pick. We had one guy end up in the hospital every year. He'd almost die from the mushrooms.

Old Man Miscola. He believed that old wive's tale—if you got a quarter or a fifty-cent piece, it doesn't matter what kind of coin you use, if you put it in the mushrooms while they were cooking, and it didn't turn black, then the mushrooms were safe.

When he'd be cooking them on top of the stove, pink, white, green mushrooms, you'd say, "Oh my God! Which ones are good?" and he'd say, "I'll show you," and he'd take a coin and put it in, and God knows what would happen with all these chemicals, and it would come out and be shiny and clean and he'd say, "It's good."

And then you'd sit down and you'd be eatin' pink, green, all kinds of mushrooms, and ah, every spring, it'd be in the newspaper. He'd be at the hospital to have his stomach pumped out and every year, people would still say, "Don't show me that trick again. We've been through this." But every year, he'd be at the hospital.

Old Man Mohawk

The janitor from a court near 18 Neptune, we called him Old Man Mohawk. I don't know if he was Indian or not, but that was the name he had. He lived on the first floor and he was always chasin' kids out of the yard, but this was a court. Old Man Mohawk, his job wasn't really takin' care of the place; it was just keepin' the kids quiet.

I remember we had this huge tree that grew out over the garage that was there and we'd climb the tree, get the branch that hung over the garage, and we'd swing out about fifty feet. Thanks God we weren't killed. The girls would do it. We'd climb the fence, jump on the tree, grab the branch, and swing out about fifty feet back and forth.

Mr. Conway owned a very respectable court next door and his tenants were very well-to-do people and here we were—troublemakers! Nothin' but kids, but it was his tree we were swingin' on, so he'd complain to Old Man Mohawk, and Old Man Mohawk would come out with a broom and he'd try to hit us as we swung by on the tree branch.

Well, one day my mother was looking out from our apartment and she saw Old Man Mohawk and he had my little sister Marilyn, and Marilyn was about ten or twelve, and he was hitting her leg as she swung by on the tree branch about fifty feet in the air. He'd jump up and try to swing the broom at her.

Now Marilyn was scared to let go, she couldn't get back to the barn and she was screaming, "Mama, Mama," and my mother looked up out the window. She was ironing, which was unfortunate, because she just pulled the iron out of the wall and "Look out now!" she threw it and got Mohawk right at the head, knocked him cold. He recovered, but he never, he never hit Marilyn again.

Theresa the Balloon Lady

Theresa the Balloon Lady, she owned a couple of houses on Buffum St. My father-in-law, he would pay money for a balloon. He might buy about one balloon for about ten kids and you'd share and that was as far as he would go because she wanted a quarter or something for a balloon. He always kind of looked through her because she was a neighborhood character, and I'll never forget his opinion changed about her, and from then on he always spoke to her.

There was this car coming down Alley St. and one of the little kids was in the street and usually the cars will go around them, but somehow this car hit this little kid, a little boy, and it pinned him by his jacket underneath the front wheel. He wasn't really hurt; he was really scared though. We didn't really know that at the time, how bad he was.

Theresa the Balloon Lady was going by, and she seen the car and the men were trying to lift the car. They didn't dare back it up because the boy was right there. Theresa the Balloon Lady, she says to Tony's father, "Here, hold these." She went over, she bent down, got underneath the fender and she lifted up that car and the men pulled the boy out.

My father-in-law from that day on, he always said, "How do you do, Theresa?" He never forgot. She could've kept right on going. She could've killed herself. She could have thrown out her back, but slowly she lifted that car until they could pull that little boy out.

—Marguerite Puleo

OUR MOTHERS-IN-LAW

1

All the Irish girls from Neptune St. would marry the Italian boys from Alley St.

I think your mother accepted me when she would serve food,
and she'd say, "I don't know if you like this or not,"
like lamb's brain with onions or, um, beef tongue,
ah, things that I had never seen or heard of before, and she'd say,
"Do you like it?" and I'd say, "Actually, I do like it. It's different,"
and then I'd say, "How do you make it? I'm gonna try it."
And from then on, it was fine.

2

I remember your mother telling me how she met your father.

She came over here first. She was only about sixteen and your father had been married before. She was working in a shoe factory and she met him and they weren't together too long before they got married.

When I married Tony, my mother-in-law was about five feet; she weighed about 250 pounds and she had big breasts and hips and she wore her hair in a bun. When we got real close and friendly, she took me upstairs in the attic there, and she opened up this old trunk, and she showed me her wedding gown.

Pure white lace, by then it turned yellow, satin, she had a little lace band, lace gloves, a veil, and she held it up and the waist was about twenty inches. And she had a switch of her hair. She was Sicilian and she had long gold-red hair that was magnificent. The switch she had must have hung down her back. She really must have been beautiful.

3

When Tony and I were starting going steady, my mother wasn't too pleased I was gonna marry an Italian fella.

I said, "Mama, give him a chance. Just meet him. See if you like him." So finally, she did give in, she invited him this Sunday, to have him for dinner. So I told Tony, I says, "Look. Be quiet." I says, "Be nice. I wanna marry you, but if my mother really says, 'No,' I'm not goin' to fight her for the rest of my life." 'Cause my mother's a spitfire. If she doesn't like you, that's it. You know it.

I say, "Just be quiet. You know she's got a very funny sense of humor. If she's laughing, enjoying you, you're in." So the only thing that stuck in his mind was that my mother had a sense of humor.

So, the house is all clean, the food's on the table, nice tablecloth, and my mother's waiting there and I says, "Mama, you're gonna like him. He's so nice, art school, college, his mother and his father own two houses."

"OK OK" A knock comes at the door. My mother opens it and there he is. He had a hat on, which he had never worn one before, a black hat, he had a long coat with the collar turned up, a cigarette drooling from his lips, and he really didn't smoke, and he says… "Ay, lady, Margie here?"

My mother's, "Oh my God! It's a Mafia. You're marrying a gangster." She took up a broom and all the way down Neptune St., every mother is looking out the door. She hit him a couple of times and he says, "I thought it was funny." My mother says, "It's not. You ever come near this house again, I'll call the police."

It took the longest time for my mother to accept him, but that *was* funny you know.

—Marguerite Puleo

BRICKYARD ARTISTS MAKE THEIR WAY

1

[Tony]: I come out of the service and on the GI Bill, I went to art school for three years. Next door neighbor there was a fella who was in Pearl Harbor. He was a sign painter and he was lettering on the ships. When they bombed them, they blew his legs off. He was doing sign painting out of his house and he got around in his wheelchair, and he did lettering, and I used to help him. And he used to say, "Hey, would you like to go to art school?" But no, I wanted to be a mechanic 'cause I worked on planes in the Navy Air Corp. So I tried three or four mechanic's schools, but I couldn't get in. So he told me about this school, Wagner School of Art in Boston. He called up and I went down to the Federal Building in Boston and registered for the GI Bill. I was getting $90 a month.

And after school, we were living on Alley and Pleasant and there was an empty store there. So I started the shop in 1950. Then from there down to Portland St., then Blossom St., then Summer St. Every time, you go in a shop, something would happen. Guy would buy the building—I gotta move. The roof would leak—I gotta move. Then I got my sign truck. I was sick and tired of being kicked out or having to leave these places.

[Marguerite]: When he first started the sign shop, there was no lack of money because the word went out that Tony is a sign painter and he didn't have to advertise. Because people come knockin' at the door.

2

[Tony]: O'Connor—he's the one who lived on Harbor St., my father's house. I went in the yard one day and there's a big donkey, life size, all tin trash cans. I said, "You do this for a hobby?" He said, "No, I've got contracts for this." I thought he's pulling my leg. But he had a whole yard full of sculptures like that.

One time, we went to the Harp & Bard on Route 1, and there in front of it was a big cart and a horse, and it was his. He sold it for about three or four thousand dollars. He made it out of all tin cans.

He worked at Lynn Storage. His daughter worked in the office and he was the custodian. So I gave him one of your *Brickyard Stories* books and he gave me three pictures of the house on Harbor St.

3

[Tony]: Joe's mother, she was deaf. She was very quiet, well, maybe because she was deaf. She didn't have anything to paint on, so what she did, in her house, the walls were just painted white, she had her whole house, she had paintings. When you came into her kitchen, one whole thing, about twelve feet long by six foot high, would be a picture of God. Just like a church. And then would be a scene where you walk into a garden.

She had no canvas. She had to paint on the walls. And it's a shame because I mean the woman was really talented. That was in the house on the first floor. And the landlord knew about it, but left the paintings alone. Self-taught. She made some of the most beautiful things. In fact, when she moved out, the people who moved in just left everything up.

15 HARBOR STREET AND 30 ALLEY STREET

1

[Tony]: When we came to Lynn, we moved to Blossom St. in a tenement. We had been there less than a year when my father saw this empty house on Harbor St. A shell, a two-family up-and-down, but there was nothin' there, no windows, no doors, just an empty shell, and my father bought it and made it all one house with a double lot—15 Harbor.

2

[Tony]: Then he got sick and tired of climbing up and down the stairs. He wanted a house all one floor. Now when he built the house on Alley St., my father was still workin' on his own. He'd come home weekends and nights and do the brick, all the masonry, it all had to be done. And then for the other work, my father'd get a carpenter.

3

[Tony]: 30 Alley. We were excavating the cellar and we were down about three feet when we realized we were gonna need to have a steam shovel come and have him do it. We were running out of time. We had to pour the foundation before winter came. It was $75, which was a lot of money, but it took him about two hours. Otherwise, it would have taken six men four weeks.

[Marguerite]: If someone was doing good work, his father would tell them. Like when Tony was cuttin' the bricks in, he'd say, "Tony, you got too much water in that cement. This is how you do it." And he'd say, "What's the difference Pa?" He says, "Because fifty years from today," he says, "I want that brick to look just like it does now."

A Baker's Dozen: Tony Puleo's Handwritten Brickyard Stories

presented below exactly as given to me before his interview on June 5. 1986

On Alley St. across my father's house was a ice truck with out wheels at night my brother and I would open a crack under the truck to get ice. The temparature was 92 degrees.

The whole street would have a party that lasted at night till 2 am a womn tenant would call the police. If you can't fight them join them. We got the woman and the polce drunk!

When the Joe Louis fight was on me and the whole neighborhood would listen to a Jew couple named Gold Berg who had the only radio on the block. By the way her daughter had a crush on me.

Down the street Mr. DiFilipino had a grape vine. On night we raided his grapes. He caught me. I grabed his leg and woul'nt let go. He finally pulled his leg away. My front tooth was stuck in his leg!

There was a mother and her black daughter named "Louise" any time she wanted attention see would yell fire, fire, fauslt alarm.

A Polish women had her 5 year old son tied on the thrd floor porch like a dog. One day we went by and smelled some meat cooking on the porch. My Brothar and I climed amed saw him eating steak. We tied him up and ate the steak.

I was the gang leader on the block 4 boys and 2 girls. No one came on my street unless we say so. Most of them had to walk the tracks. Including my future wife!

Any time some one stole or broke something the cop on the beat Mr. Crowley would bribe us with candy or money to find who did it. We always blamed Jew boy Louis.

One July 4, - old man Murphy who had a wooden leg would sleep on the porch. We lit a "4" inch bomb and blew his wooden leg off!

A Irish old man wouldn't let us play on the sidewalk in front of his house. So, when his Ford car was parked in front of the house. we got a long roop and tied it to his axle. When he pulled away the front porch and his tentent who was sleeping at the time was half way down the street

Sat. was time to go to the movies the Automobile Theater cost 11 cents. We would steal tires from the junkie and sell them back to him

Our next door neighbor had chickens – we would take one, pluck all the feathers and throw them back into her yard, we said her dog ate it

A Gipsy family moved in next door. For 3 months they never paid for electric bill or water bill because they hooked into the 2nd floor meters

Judy Christian & Chris Maniatis Remember Their Father: Darrell O'Connor

CHRIS AND JUDY'S BRICKYARD

1

[Judy]: We enjoyed living in the Brickyard because my dad was a little famous there. Kids would come after school just to see the goats and see all of the tin works that we had in our yard. The fence around the house was all hand painted with flowers and fancy decorations.

[Chris]: One of the things I remember was if you got in a cab any time, you could say, "I live in the house with the tin sculpture," and they knew just where to go.

[Judy]: A lot of times the high school kids would come and put their friends out in front of one of the statues if they'd had a little bit too much to drink and then they'd wake up underneath the tin man or the dragon and it was pretty fun.

2

[Chris] My dad bought the house from Mr. Puleo who lived in the house behind us, who had come from Italy, and he had built our house on Harbor St. from scratch. 'Cause he had a bunch of kids and he rented the house. The house was vacant for a long time, but when my father came and he saw he had eight kids and he says, "You know what? You can have the house." And he let him buy that house from him directly. Fifteen dollars a week until it was paid for. And that's how the neighborhood was back then.

3

[Judy]: When we first moved there, there was a boarding house on the corner of the street, and then two apartments, houses, one front, one back, that the woman just went back to Italy and left them behind. There was no furniture or anything. They were just derelict. And then Pudgy's came in and tore 'em all down. The tenement there, the boarding house, burned down and Pudgy's bought the property and built the store. George Nelson bought the property on the other side of us and had a little welding shop.

Our Front Yard on Harbor Street

1

[Chris]: This is a picture of our front yard on Harbor St. and you can see the dragon and there was a, I guess you'd call it a bug, and the tin man right here, and in the back, that's me and my father. It was all the front yard because on Harbor St., the house was the furthest thing back. And then there was the grapevine, and in front of the grapevine was the fence, and the tin man was there, and another little creature he had there, and you could go up to it and it would talk to you. There was a big giant, a huge giant, and we had a caterpillar on a mushroom. And some of them would move in the wind.

And then we had a big like six- or eight-foot-high fence, and it would go all the way down, and it was made out of masonite or something, sheets all together so that we couldn't see the junkyard, and it was all painted with all different kinds of things. And the mailbox would be your giraffe. And the goats were down where the witch was. The witch was on top of the goat house, which was made out of an old Volkswagen car, and it would cackle as well. So, it was pretty fun. Then he would have his workshop: he had an old school bus in the back. Real live goats. We had live goats in the yard. That was in the *Item*.

2

[Judy]: I remember we had a little garden in the yard with corn and tomatoes and things. One morning my father runs in and says, "Get up! Get up!" at five o'clock in the morning, and Barchy's horses were in the garden eatin' all the corn stalks. It was the mother and the pony and they cleaned the garden down to the stubs. We're all climbing on my father's bed to look out the window and we broke his bed. When you got eight kids all hangin' on one bed, it was enough. So it was fun. We enjoyed it a lot.

[Chris]: Barchy's horses would come and visit us every once in a while. At that time, they could kind of wander a little free 'cause there wasn't that much car traffic.

C. BAIN

1

[Judy]: C. Bain was on Pleasant St. across the street from our house. When I applied for a job there in 1968, it was the old Lynn Storage warehouse. And I had to look it up on the map, 'cause I didn't know where it was, and it was around the corner. So you went out past Pudgy's across the street and there it was. It's still there, that giant white storage building. And I've worked there since 1968. And when Bain bought the building, I was still there. And I went with them to Linden St. and then Peabody, but I'm not goin' to Methuen. That's too far, that's why I took the job in the first place—'cause it was close to home.

We were thankful that eventually everybody in my family: my sister, my brother Matt helped paint the building, my brother Tim, my brother Darrell, who helped a little bit too, but Matt and my father worked there the longest, and Chris and myself. I was the first one there, but it just worked out. It was like they were a family business and they all seemed to stick with family people if they could. When you've got a loyal person in a family and the rest want to come, it worked.

At C. Bain, my father could repair anything. He was a cabinet maker in his youth, so damaged furniture, claims from customers about artwork, I know he repaired some artwork for Harvard University, so sculptures and things that got damaged, they would repair them so that they would look pretty original by the time he got done. He would take care of the buildin', repair furniture, build crates, make signs, whatever they needed, he could do it.

2

[Chris]: My father also decorated restaurants. He had his metal sculptures out in front of the Harp & Bard in Peabody and he decorated the inside. And the Harp & Bard at that time was a big draw for the hockey players—the Boston Bruins used to go there all the time and my father would get to meet all of the players. They all knew who he was.

He did The Landing in Marblehead and he did that place in Boston—Cheers—he designed the sign and he designed a lot of the artwork inside. So, he was pretty famous in his own right. And of course, he painted the C. Bain building, painted it, repaired it, him and my brothers. To us he was famous. And he's been in a lot of magazines, Yankee Magazine, an interview with Channel 2, and one of his sculptures is at the Lynn Museum, a metal Boston terrier dog that actually was on a postcard when they were advertising something.

A Good Elm Farms Story

[Judy]: My father also had chickens. Now Elm Farms was the first supermarket that had the open, you step on the mat and the door opened for you. Well, one day the police come to the house, and they have a chicken, a rooster, in the back seat of the car. And they told my father, "Will you please keep the rooster in the yard because he's up at the Elm Farms pecking the people trying to go in the door." He said an old guy's trying to go in, the guy's got a cane, the bird's chasin' him, and tryin' to get into the supermarket.

And then a couple of weeks later, we found the chicken bones over near the hoboes' place across the street. The rooster disappeared a couple of weeks before. We never saw him again. We used to call 'em the hoboes; they used to have their campfire across the street. It was all vacant back then and they'd be over there havin' a campfire. You weren't afraid. It was just part of where you were.

[Chris]: They used to live on the tracks. You'd see 'em over on the tracks but every once in a while, they'd be over in the fields. But there was a lot of vacant property down there back at that time. There used to be a motorcycle shop across the street from our house, and then one night they just disappeared with all the motorcycles. They couldn't find them after that. So it was kind of a busy neighborhood. Hood's was still there, and we'd see the trains parked up at Hood's, so all the homeless people, or whatever they were at the time, would hang out over there.

Our Front Yard in the *Item*

[Chris]: Here's a newspaper article from *The Lynn Item*, May 21, 1969. It's called, "Darrell O'Connor Creates Lynn 'Land of Oz.'" Listen to this part:

> O'Connor, an accomplished artist and sculptor, created this wonderland for children, not only for his own eight, but for the many others who, through the years, have derived indescribable joy from viewing the antics of the live animals and imagining the meanderings of the others.
>
> O'Connor has used every type of scrap metal in constructing the creatures. The fact that the O'Connor home is in close proximity to several junk yards has facilitated his task, since it has been possible to pick up 'ears,' 'noses,' and 'eyes' from a pile of junk.
>
> What are some of the component parts of the creatures? Milk cans, hot water tanks, hub caps, stovepipes, water pipes, oil drums,

tin cans, oil can covers, furnaces and other assorted items have been cleverly utilized by O'Connor in the creation of each creature.

The witch flying in front of the O'Connor porch is also equipped with a built-in intercom system, which is operated from the O'Connor's living room. Children are now used to shouting to the witch and hearing her reply.

The tin woodsman is a remarkable likeness of the character from "The Wizard of Oz." His hat is a large funnel and the face has been so expertly created as to be almost life-like. Other parts of the woodsman are stove pipes and a small oil drum. At night he looks positively alive.

The giant is composed of a 50-gallon oil drum for a torso and two hot water tanks for legs. The beanie he wears is part of a weathervane salvaged by O'Connor from the cupola of a demolished building.

EXILE AND RETURN

1

[Chris]: Then I think he had to move the stuff because of thieves, which I don't remember that. Then someone wrote another article and it says, "The gaily painted works of Darryl O'Connor no longer grace the streets of the junkyards. Where has he gone, the whimsical wizard of sculpture?"

2

[Judy]: He left in '69. Eminent domain came in and took the land. He couldn't buy a place here for the money they gave him so he had to move to New Hampshire, and he stayed there for 30 years, '69–'86, and then he moved back to Hanover St., and he still had artwork all over the house.

3

[Chris]: This picture is of the front of his house and every single window has a cut-out. The top ones were from Alice in Wonderland, all cut-outs of Alice in Wonderland, and then he had masks and all kinds of cut-outs—every window—you could see the hex signs on the top of the house. The Spanish people would come by and cross the street instead of walking in front of my father's house. He had chicken feet hangin' in the windows and artwork, his monster masks and things that he made.

HURRICANE CAROL 1954

[Judy]: We lived on Church St., and at the end of the street, it was a dead end. The train wall was there. And the hurricane came and we lived at right near Blood's building. OK. And the rain filled that street. It was so full, and then when it stopped rainin' and you look out and all the people're in the water. If you could believe it. Those people were splashin' around, playin' in that water like it was a swimmin' pool. It was like, are you kiddin' me? But, that's how it was. Soon as that rain stopped, they were out there jumpin' around, and havin' a good ol' time ya know.

[Chris]: That's when we got our first tv and they had Kennedy's peanut butter. I can still remember. There was a big Kennedy store. I can still remember that day. We had Kennedy's peanut butter and we were watchin' tv, and then the storm came and the next thing you know, people are out swimmin' in the water. Today, you'd die from that! Back in that day, it didn't matter.

ENTERTAINMENT AND ENTERTAINERS

When it came to Christmas
like on my street
there was a lot of Jewish people
so there was no lights
but as soon as you went over
to Blossom St.
it was just so beautiful
all the people's lights

—Delores Jackson

Chick Gecoya's *Remembrances* and Kathryn Grover's history contain many descriptions of what Brickyarders did for entertainment. Since money was scarce, most entertainments were free or low-cost. Games like Peggy, which was played using sticks, took place in the streets. Movies were very popular, as were athletic clubs that fielded baseball and football teams and provided facilities for boxing.

Some pranks became well-known sources of amusement in the neighborhood. A tire tied to a rope might be put on a street and when a motorist stopped to pick it up, someone hiding would tug on the rope, keeping the tire out of the reach of the frustrated patsy. "Yoo-hoo May" was a more elaborate prank in which a gullible male outsider would agree to bring a gift to a supposedly eligible young woman only to be frightened by a threatening father figure into dropping the gift and running away.

Brickyarders were also entertainers. Movie and television actors Walter Brennan, Jack Albertson and Telly Savalas were said to have come out of the Brickyard. The stories in this brief section provide a glimpse into the world of entertainment in the Brickyard and are told by these speakers:

Edward McDonald (1919–____)

I interviewed Ed in his home in Lynn on May 4, 1982. Ed was a descendant of the Alley family, who were among the first residents of the original Brickyard. His wife Mary was part of the Summer Circle Association, a group of women who met monthly to reminisce about the Brickyard and to whom I was introduced by Evelyn Lazaris. After World War II, Edward took advantage of the GI Bill to move out of the Brickyard, and he served as a firefighter in Lynn for many years. A practical man, he used to say, "When you don't have a lot, it doesn't take a heck of a lot to make you happy."

Lou Amico, known professionally as Lou Ames (1913–2001)

When I interviewed Lou on May 26, 1982 at the Lou Ames Music Store on Union St. in Lynn, he had been in business there for a quarter century. His parents came to Lynn from Cartenesta, Italy, and his father Salvatore opened the first Italian meat market and grocery in Lynn on the corner of Pleasant St. and Summer St. One of Lou's proudest accomplishments was starting the Professional Musicians Club of the North Shore, an organization devoted to helping musicians in need. The story of his career as a professional musician spans a half century, and the arc of the story of his band playing summer concerts on Lynn Common parallels the story of the Brickyard in the 50s, 60s and 70s.

Edward McDonald

THE CIRCUS COMES TO LYNN

When we were kids—
now if my kid did it, I'd brain him—
we would go out and stay out all night long
and we'd tell our parents it was because
the circus was coming to town.

We'd go to the railway and watch the circus come in.
They take all the wagons off the flatcars
and the elephants would pull 'em
and then they'd take them up to Barry Park through the streets
and then we'd get a job feeding the elephants or watering them
to get a free ticket to the circus.

There was more fun then than today.

See, before, there were many interesting things to see.
Now, if you want to go to the circus,
you got to fight the traffic to get into Boston Garden
and go into a moldy old building to watch it.

When I grew up, it was outside and you could stand around
and watch all the performers eat in a tent.

It was really interesting.

Lou Ames

Starting My Trumpet Career

I couldn't have been more than ten years old
and I lived on South St.
We lived in the front house
and in the back house lived a trumpet player.
I used to hear him play when he practiced
and I liked what I heard.

So I used to go up on Federal St.
and look in a pawn shop window at a bugle,
just a regulation bugle that cost $3.50.
And to get that $3.50, I sold rags
to the junkman and collected bottles.
I made sachet and sold it
for ten cents a package.
And I bought the bugle and had fun with it.

And as time went on, I was able to get
a little job here and there and then
we moved to Tremont St.,
right next door to Jerome DelCampo
who became my teacher.
I started my trumpet career at twelve years old.
When I got my first trumpet,
which cost me twenty dollars,
it took me a year to pay for it.
And I took lessons from Jerome.
And then I took lessons from a place in Central Square
and then I went to the New England Conservatory.

VERY HECTIC TIMES DURING THAT BIG DEPRESSION

1

I joined the John H. Casey Big Band
and we started off barnstorming
and seldom did we come home
with more than two dollars for a day's pay.

I can remember very very vividly one job
just to give you an idea of what it was like.
We went all the way to Skowhegan, Maine,
which is about two hundred or more miles away.
Admission was 25 cents to the dance hall
and they didn't make enough to pay the band
so we came back with maybe a dollar and a half,
two dollars in our pockets.
It cost us more than we made to go up there and back.

We had to leave early in the morning.
In those days they didn't have the big highways like today.
We got back home the next morning at 7:00
just in time to freshen up and jump in the cars—
we used a couple of cars to carry the whole band—
and go off on another job
which was in Gardner.
Today, Gardner is maybe a one-hour drive
but in those days it was five or six.
And the same thing happened:
after two days
when we came home
we had no money.

The money that we made
we had to spend for sandwiches
and things like that,
gasoline for the cars and all that jazz.
And this is what went on during the Depression.

2

One time we went down to play
at the Roseland Ballroom in Taunton.
The same thing—
the admission was about 25 cents,
but we only had about ten or fifteen people show up.
Rose Chaplin was the manager
and she was a very very nice person.
And at the end of the evening, we're packed up,
and she comes over and says, "What can I tell you?
Go in the kitchen and whatever you can find
you can eat."
And that was our pay for that night.
It was very hectic times during that big Depression.

3

And as time went by, the big band era faded.
Beano took over.
Instead of the dancing, Beano.
The big dance halls were now Beano
and the people,
instead of spending a quarter to dance,
they try to make fifty cents or a dollar from their quarter.

So we jacked the big band
and went into small band work.
This was the early 30s.
I would say 1933 because I remember
our first job in Boston as a small club band.
We played on Franklin St.
It was the—um…
what was the name of that place?
… it was just a small restaurant…
a four-piece band and for the first time,
we were able to take home
what we considered decent pay
which was eighteen dollars a week.

But we worked all day and all night for it.
We played a noon session, 12:00 to 2:00.
Then we played supper, which was 5:00 to 7:00,
and then we came back at eight o'clock
and played until 1:00 in the morning

… eighteen hours… seven days a week
no no… that one was six days… six days a week.

Gee, I can't think of the name of that restaurant.

4

And from there we bounced around.
We played all the Chinese joints in Boston.
You name 'em, we played 'em.
There were a lot of places in Chinatown that offered music
and the same hours—12:00 to 2:00, 5:00 to 7:00 and 8:00 to 1:00.

There was one place called The Red Rooster
and from there we moved to the big place
down on Huntington Avenue
across from the New England Conservatory;
it was called the… ah…
I can't remember the name of that one either.

Then we really made it big.
We went and played the Lido
in Boston on Warrenton St.
across from the Metropolitan Theater.
The Lido was a very big, nice, club-type Chinese restaurant.
The stage was built in tiers
and we had a six-piece band there.
That was a very nice gig, but it was short-lived.
It seemed like every time we went into a place,
while it was still Depression,
come New Year's Eve, it would close.

The last place that we played
and everybody will remember the Palladium in Boston,
Huntington Avenue, and the big name
that played there for years was Jimmy Gallagher.
He used to be on the air every night about midnight
and they would say, "Jimmy Gallagher—still hanging on."
Well, Jimmy Gallagher finally went out—
and we came in and then the same thing.
We were in there about three months—
then come New Year's Eve, they folded,
and instead of pay, the fella says,
"Help yourselves. Whatever you see,
you want it, take it home."

We didn't feel bad about closing places
and I'll tell you why.
Everybody was in the same boat.
Things were bad.
Things were real bad.
So we didn't feel bad about it.
As a matter of fact, we used to joke about it:
"Well, I wonder how long we're going to be in here
before it closes."

PLAYING ALL THE BIG ACTS

1

The big break was 1938.
I remember very vividly.
From the Lido, we went into the… no…
don't tell me… Lowell…
the New American Hotel in Lowell,
a restaurant-type room that was fantastic.
The Depression was beginning to pass,
and things were beginning to look better.
We booked that one for thirty dollars a week each
which was big money in those days.
And the hours were good.
We had rehearsal and the show went on at nine o'clock
and the second show was 10:30 and we played 'til 1:00.
So it was a short, short hour job,
considering what we had been doing.
It was a fantastic job,
the most memorable one in my whole life.

We're playing the shows and the dancing.
Our piano player's name was George Clark Brockett
and my name of course was Lou Amico
so we named the band Lou Clark.

We played all the big acts
all the big acts
and some of them went on to Hollywood
and became very famous.

Billy DeWolfe— remember him?
Then there's one that's on tv now: "Shirley and Laverne"
DeFazio... DeFazio the father he played
and... and... Yolanda and Valez—the million-dollar dance team
they were tops... we played them.

2

Eric Rhodes was another movie star.
We played him at the Mayfair Club here in Lynn.
The stars usually did twenty or thirty minutes.
And of course there were the emcees.
The biggest emcee in the North Shore area was Freddie Ross,
who also came from the Brickyard.
There was a famous midgets band
famous throughout the world and we played them
at the Capitol Theater in Lynn—
Hermime's Midgets Band
—now wait a minute—
we played them at the Lucerne Café
which was right here in Central Square.
In the 40s I went into the Lucerne
because of the gas rationing.
We couldn't get around.
And there again at the Lucerne
we played for top acts.

3

During the war, the Lucerne was The Spot.
I went in there with my little group in '42
and I stayed until '46.
Then on V-J Day,
it was summer and it was warm, so they
opened the double doors in the back
because the air conditioning wasn't working.
Now I'm not gonna mention whether it was Marines
or Navy men or regular Army men,
but evidently they started calling each other names
and they started a fight
and the fight was just like in the movies.
It started up at the tables
and ended up on the dance floor.

And I got up and played "The Star-Spangled Banner"
'cause that makes them stop and they salute.
But they didn't stop at all.
They kept on fighting.
There must have been four or five pairs
of guys fighting like crazy.
And they fought themselves right out into the street
through those big open doors
and then they closed the doors and the fight was outside
and then the cops came and took care of it.
That was something else—something to remember.

4

Then there was the Golden Anchor.
I went in there in '46,
a year after the war was over,
and I stayed until '52.
This was the Golden Anchor in Danvers
which was known as the...
ah, how did they bill that now?
Well, it was the most modern night club on the North Shore.
It had a sliding stage, which nobody had.
They were the first ones.

When it's show time, you press a button
and this sliding stage comes out over the dance floor
and the show would be up on that platform
so that everyone in the room
no matter where they were sitting
they could see.

And here again, we played all the top acts.
My biggest thrill was when Charley Spivak came in
with his singer and he would come up on the bandstand
and do some numbers with us and we'd have a ball.
Charley Spivak was a trumpet player,
The Sweetest Trumpet Player This Side of...
of... what was it? Oh my, what was it?
The Sweetest Trumpet Player This Side of...
of something. I forget,
but that's what they called him.
Not only did the Golden Anchor have the sliding stage,
but they had tremendous shows, tremendous shows.
That's where we played DeFazio

from "Laverne and Shirley."
That's where we played him.

THE LOU AMES MARCHING BAND AND SUMMER CONCERTS ON THE COMMON

1

For the last appearance of the Lou Ames Marching Band on the street,
I called the papers and said, "I don't know if it's of any interest but…"
That was November 1978.
I had the marching band for 32 years.
I was a young fella when I took it over in '46
from the vice-president of the musician's union local 126.
He was the director of the band and I played solo trumpet for him.
Richard Townsend started the band in 1936
and because of ill health, he had to quit,
so I told him I enjoyed playing with the band
and that I'd like to carry it on under his name
and he said, "I'm glad you came up. Out of all the guys that would offer,
I was hoping it would be you, but you don't put it under my name.
You put your name."
And that's how the Lou Ames Marching Band came about.
There were 25 in the band, and as the prices went up,
we had to decrease the number
until we wound up with a 20-piece band on the street.

When I took the marching band over
and we went down the street playing "The St. Louie Blues March,"
the old-timers didn't like us new guys coming into their territory,
so they made a complaint to the Park Commission in Lynn
and told them I was playing jazz on the street on a marching job.
And I was called in before the Commission
and they wanted to know if I'd actually played jazz on the street.
I said, "No. I'm not playing jazz on the street. Why?"
"You're playing 'The St. Louie Blues'."
I said, "I was playing 'The St. Louie Blues March.'
Glenn Miller played that overseas during the war as a march
and he wrote it as a march and if he played it as a march,
then we can do the same thing, can't we?"
They agreed: "OK Lou, you win."
And that took care of the narrow-minded old-timers.

2

George Klangos was a barber on Summer St.
and in his will he asked for a marching band to play his funeral
and his widow picked my band to do that.
And it became a big big thing.
It hit the *Strange as it Seems* column and that was in *The Detroit Times*.
This thing went national. 1952.
At the time, it was just another marching job
but then geesh—we come down Pleasant St.
and you see all these movie cameras and people taking pictures
and I say, "What the heck is going on?"
I didn't realize until then that this is a big thing around here.
This was only known down South where they used to have
funeral marches with the band in back.
Jazz actually, they played jazz.
So it was a big thing to have something like that happen here in the North.

3

And then once again, I was called in before the Park Commission.
They were saying I was playing jazz on the bandstand on the Common.
This was a few years after that first time.
So I went down to them and explained I was not playing jazz,
and that I am not a jazz trumpet player.
I was playing the same songs the other bands were playing on the bandstand,
only with a modern arrangement.
They're playing waltzes. I'm playing waltzes.
They're playing the pop songs of today; I'm playing the pop songs of today.
It's not jazz.

4

The bandstand concerts were on the Common,
Wednesday nights during the summer,
and we were one of several bands that played them.
The concerts went very very well when I first started.
I was the first one in the area to have a dance band
and a piano within a concert band.
And the Common had the fountain with the colored lights.
On Wednesday night they put the watercolors on
and it was beautiful. Beautiful.
It was, if I'm correct, the only watercolors around this area,

and so people would gather and watch the watercolors
while they listened to the music.

And as the years went on, vandalism took care of the watercolors
and they got to the point where they couldn't be used any more.
And then in later years, muggers began making it hard
for the older people to come out.
They loved to come down to hear the concerts,
and they'd be out 'til ten o'clock at night,
but then they wouldn't go because they were getting mugged.
And I hate to say this—not too much police protection.
As a matter of fact, sometimes I had to go over
to the telephone across the street and call up the police department
to send some cops down
because the kids were being unruly and throwing rocks.
This is in the 70s.

Then they would send the police down there,
but I don't know why they didn't do it every week.
Now you can't blame the police too much.
I think at that time they weren't being paid for overtime
and that was an overtime job.
After all, if they come out and do four, five hours work,
they should get paid for it.
I don't think they settled that until just recently,
but that was the end of the concerts on the Common.
It got to the point where the band outnumbered the audience.
It was the muggings that made the people afraid to come out.
We even changed the time from 8:00 to 10:00 to 7:00 to 9:00
and that didn't help.

Things started to go downhill in the 50s
and it got worse in the 60s
and by the 70s it was over.

LASTING ATTACHMENTS

Until I left Lynn in 1942, I had never been further west than Barry Park, north of Boston St. or east of Fisherman's Beach. But it was a narrower range than that.

People around had cars, especially bootleggers, but most of us walked. You lived in the context of what and where you could travel to by foot. It tended to heighten the sense of common humanity, of shared experience.

Everyone was poor in a way that is not understood today. There is a kind of banality in the claim that no-one realized how deprived they were, because there was nothing to compare with, no television, no demented consumerism...

All the kids going to college on the GI Bill were spurred by a work ethic rooted in an awareness of deprivation that was illuminated by realizing how close to real disaster all of us truly were.

It was always in our minds like an unforgiving arctic wasteland. Our kids don't know what we are talking about.

—From a letter sent to me by Harry Rosenthal dated May 14, 1986. Harry Rosenthal was a textile artist and designer. In his youth, he lived in the Brickyard on Olsen Terrace.

To paraphrase a popular saying, you can leave the Brickyard, but the Brickyard never leaves you. As Kathryn Grover noted in the title of her history, the Brickyard lives on in the legends told about it, but it's more than that. The Brickyard lives on in the manner having lived there influences the ongoing lives of its former residents. That influence can express itself in a variety of ways as these storytellers in this section show:

Arnold Trachtman (1930–2019)

I interviewed Arnold in my kitchen on August 9, 2001. He was a graduate of Massachusetts College of Art and he received his MFA from The Art Institute of Chicago. Arnold was a progressive activist throughout his life and many of his paintings show his distaste for fascism, Nazism and authoritarianism. In the late 1970s, he became part of the Lynn Voices Collaborative with photographer Peter Bates and poet Bill Costley. They published two broadsides included in *The Newspaper,* a short-lived independent Lynn monthly, they were featured in an issue of the journal *Radical America* and they participated in several Celebrations of the Poetry of Lynn held at North Shore Community College.

Arnold is considered one of the Boston Expressionists, his paintings have been shown in galleries across New England and the Boston Public Library has a large collection of his work in its permanent collection. I own two of his paintings, one from a series of seven Lynn cityscapes, and the other, "Mr. Tillson Makes His Way Through the Brickyard," which is on the cover of this book.

The Three of Us: Jeanette Carter, Flora Epps (1927–2011), Doris Harewood (1929–2019)

These lifelong friends graduated from Lynn Classical High School in the years following World War II, and for the next forty years, they got together regularly to talk, catch up and carry on. On July 25, 1986, I was invited into their circle of conversation to share in their memories of the Brickyard. Unfortunately, it's sometimes hard to identify which of the three is speaking on the recording I made of that morning's proceedings. The three laugh, they interrupt, they comment and they respond to each other. I've done my best, and I hope I haven't confused or mistaken any speakers, and if I have, my sincere apologies. Because of this possibility, the first and the last two stories in this series are best considered told by a composite of the voices of The Three of Us.

Ruth Tansey (1927–   )

On August 12, 2019, I interviewed Ruth in her apartment at St. Mary's Plaza on Pleasant St. Before going over there, I had breakfast with her son Russ Tansey and her nephew Ralph Tufo. Russ told me his mom had her hair done for the interview, and to me, this said all there was to say about how important the Brickyard is to her.

Delores Jackson (1935–   )

I interviewed Delores Jackson in her home on March 25, 2019. I had met her earlier that month at the Lynn Museum and was excited to learn that her mother, Gladys Haywood, lived for a time in the Brickyard house once inhabited by Jan Matzeliger, the inventor of the lasting machine, which revolutionized shoe manufacturing. Gladys was among those instrumental in ensuring that

Matzeliger's memory and achievement would be permanently preserved, most notably by the issuance of a commemorative stamp in his honor by the U.S. Post Office, the fourteenth in the Black Heritage series. On September 15, 1991, Gladys spoke at the stamp's First Day of Issue ceremony, held at the Lynn Museum near the Matzeliger exhibit.

Gordon Laro (1939–2003)

Gordon was working as a custodian at the Beverly, MA campus of North Shore Community College when I interviewed him there on December 1 and 8, 1986. During our conversations, he told me about how his father loved to hunt and fish and how he carried his dad from room to room in their home after he was partially paralyzed in a workplace accident. Gordon also carried around Dicky Landry, the legendary Brickyard child who lost his legs in a train mishap. Gordon is a quintessential Brickyarder. From a racially and ethnically diverse background, he was a hard worker devoted to his family. A long-time resident of Summer Circle, on Sundays he went back to the Brickyard to the corner store on Alley St. to pick up the paper and shoot the breeze with other guys from the Brickyard.

Eleanor Fisher (1940–   )

I interviewed Eleanor on the patio of her home in Lynn's Diamond District overlooking Lynn Beach on June 10, 1986. Eleanor had a career as a psychotherapist and as a young woman once won the "Mrs. Massachusetts" pageant. In recent years, she has become a glass-shard painter; her work can be seen on her website: <www.eleanorfisher.net>. What is striking about Eleanor's Brickyard stories is how they are driven by the feelings she associates with her memories.

Paul Benson (1946–   )

I interviewed Paul at his home in Peabody, MA on July 1, 2019. He had a career with the Massachusetts Department of Corrections and was also an Adjunct Professor of History at North Shore Community College. A few books about Lynn history sat on a table beside us and Paul sometimes referred to them as he spoke.

Arnold Trachtman

ARNOLD TRACHTMAN'S BRICKYARD

1

The Brickyard was the real world. I never could leave it behind even if I tried. I was always there. My mother would say, "You always paint garbage barrels." What else would I see? It's my ground, my grounding, where I feel comfortable.

2

Take the man in the foreground of my recent painting, "Mr. Tillson Makes His Way Through the Brickyard." He was an Orthodox Jew who dressed like an Orthodox Jew. He was a glazier; you broke a window, you'd call him up. He would come over and do a magnificent job. You'd often see him walking through the streets carrying a piece of glass on his way to a job.

The way he looked was fascinating. Most of the people who worked with their hands did not have beards or dress in such a formal way. He reminded me of Michelangelo's Moses. Of course, he was less terrifying. He had a magnificent beard and mustache. He was very handsome, sort of squarish. He had an even temper; he was an even sort of person. He went to an Orthodox synagogue on Shepard St., and once in a while I saw him coming from there. He was a figure in the neighborhood.

THE TRICK TO BEING JEWISH IN THE BRICKYARD

1

I was forced to go to Hebrew school. Some years ago, in an old trunk, I actually found a diploma from Hebrew school. My parents were not actively religious. However, they felt very Jewish. It was almost a racial thing.

Temple was for the upper classes. It was on Green St. In the Brickyard, there were Reform synagogues and Orthodox synagogues. We went sporadically to a Reform synagogue on the official holidays. Temple was for the Swampscott crowd, the people who made it. At least that was our view of it. It was probably fairly accurate.

Also, I must say the Jews in the area were very very clannish. They sort of stuck together. It was very weird if you had a non-Jewish friend in those days because you couldn't trust them. That was the world. I had a few; I didn't bring any home. It was like that. If I did, my mother would be perfectly polite to them. It was like that.

2

It was tricky to be Jewish in the Brickyard. At any time or anywhere you could come under threat or attack. A particular nemesis were the parochial school kids who you could spot a mile away in their little black suits. We could see them coming up the streets.

You know, we'd come out of the movies and we'd see a couple of them coming down the street and they'd throw a challenge at you like, "Hey, Jewboy!" I'd be furious. I didn't know how to fight. I was never taught to fight. My father as a young man was an amateur boxer, but he didn't teach me a damn thing about boxing. He didn't want me to have anything to do with it.

So, the working strategy was to talk your way out of a fight or to ignore it or to run away, but I couldn't do that, so I took beatings until finally I decided it was time to learn how to defend myself. I was about twelve or thirteen and there was a Jewish Community Center and they were giving boxing and wrestling lessons, useful skills for a Jewish boy. I came to be pretty good as a boxer. I trained seriously, not that I thought I'd be a fighter, but I liked the discipline, going regularly to the gym, punching the bag, occasionally sparring with somebody. I liked the training better than the fighting actually.

3

And one memorable fight that I had started with the usual provocative "Hey Jewboy!" sort of thing. The fight began after school at Cobbet Junior High. It started and a teacher broke it up. It was the day that Roosevelt died, a hot day for April, unseasonably hot. The fight got stopped before it really got started, and that night I went to the Boy's Club on the Common next to the Public Library.

It had a swimming pool, one of the few places where you could go swimming, and sure enough, the damn guy was there. So we decided to continue the fight on the Common. Can you believe it? He didn't have a chance. He was a big guy, but he really didn't know how to box, and I was really doing him up. He was bleeding from all sorts of places and at one point I said, "I quit. That's enough." He was boring. It was just boring. And I don't think I had a serious fight after that.

Becoming an Artist

1

I was not terribly interested in high school. Lynn Classical High School was a jock school. We had that marvel Harry Agganis. He was extraordinarily talented and that didn't leave much room for a lesser athlete. And like anybody my size, I was practically required to play football. But I was big and clumsy and myopic, and that along with my lack of coordination at age fifteen contributed to my failure. And I had feet so big they couldn't even find cleats for me.

2

But all the time I was drawing and painting. I knew I wanted to be an artist, but I didn't know how. There was no one among my parents and the people I met who had a clue. There were the clichés you saw in Hollywood movies, which was the artist in the garret or the artist living in some fashionable studio apartment with beautiful northern light. But no artist that I have ever known lived like that.

I'd go for rides with my uncle through Boston and we'd see all these marvelous things—the Everett gas tanks, big lighted globes, the Narrow Gauge railway—all sorts of marvelous things for a kid. I was goggle-eyed at all this stuff, and I wanted to somehow express that, and as a kid I experienced a lot of frustration that I couldn't quite do it yet. But I kept trying.

My parents didn't know what to do with me. They'd buy me paints; they'd buy me crayons. I'd work on something and it didn't come out the way I wanted it and I'd throw a tantrum, start kicking a wall. They'd say, "Well don't do it if it disturbs you and makes you crazy." I couldn't stop. I just knew that I liked to make pictures and I wanted to always make pictures. That's what helped me to understand the world; really, it was a tool for understanding.

3

I was not a very successful reader in those days. I became a better reader with the help of a mentor friend who was an excellent teacher. He was about five years older than I was when I met him on my first job. I was making thirty cents an hour as a soda jerk at a drugstore on Summer St. called Sheldon's Pharmacy. He was a doctor's son and had an interest in music. He represented a different class.

He came from a petite-bourgeoisie family with enough comfort so they could think of the finer things in life like art and music and stuff like that. I was literally a working-class kid and I was lucky if I could find a book around the house. He opened up a whole world to me. He loaned me art books and took me to Boston.

I'd never been to Boston without my mother and he took me to art museums. It was exciting and I caught the bug to go into Boston. In high school, I began to see a lot of this guy and he introduced me to people in Lynn who were interested in art. I would never have met them, well maybe I would have, but I was sort of a blundering kid.

4

I became a real culture vulture. I became interested in plays and back then you could actually afford to go see plays and I saw as many as I could afford. I saw "Oklahoma" in Boston. I really felt I was joining a new class.

In a funny way, in order to become an artist, I had to betray the class I was born into. You sort of have to say, "I can't do that anymore. I can't hang out with the boys." Those people were always putting me down and now it was my turn to put them down. It was a sort of reverse snobbery. I was moving from the working class into the middle class, a place where artists were appreciated.

And one of the things I did in high school in self-defense was to initiate the four-day week at school. On the fifth day, I would take the bus into Boston and go to see a foreign film. At that time, foreign films were just coming into this country and there were a number of art theaters that showed them exclusively, mostly French and Italian. The routine was to go in, have lunch in a Chinese restaurant and go to the movies.

5

Although I didn't have role models, it was possible then to become an artist if you came from the working class. Today, it's very unusual for someone from the working class to aspire to become an artist. I think the Depression was the great leveler and that was a period where people from the working class could become great artists.

Two examples are Jack Levine and Hyman Bloom, both of whom came from Boston and were prodigies taken under the wing of Denman Ross of Harvard. He was a professor emeritus and for a while he gave both of them a stipend to work with him. They came from immigrant Jewish families. The people who came after that were a little too late.

Coming from a working-class background puts you at a disadvantage in the art world because you come with a different sensibility. You don't come to confirm the art world's point of view; you come to confirm yours and that sort of makes you an outsider immediately. People that buy art want to see themselves reflected in it and that becomes a problem in a career of someone with a working-class perspective.

After high school, I went to Mass Art, the only state art school in the country, and in those days you could go there for a hundred dollars a year. Can you believe that? And if you signed on for the education program, which I didn't, you could go for seventy dollars a year. It was a state normal school, but it had a fine arts division, which is what I wanted.

In the meantime my parents are saying, "How are you going to support yourself? How are you going to make a living?" That was a constant theme. I lived in Lynn for 2½ years of the four I was at Mass Art, and then I moved to Boston.

URBAN RENEWAL

On Summer St., within a triangle of just a few blocks,
there were three Jewish bakeries.
Three!
There was the New York Model,
there was the Lynn Baking Co.,
and there was Stone's.

Summer St. was a vibrant commercial area,
full of little grocery stores, candy stores, barber shops,
Chinese laundries, fish markets, and one of the first Stop & Shops
was there between Blossom and Shepard St.

It started out as a comparatively smallish place called Rabinowitz's
and then they knocked that flat and there was a big hole in the ground
and I remember I was still going to the Washington Community School
and it was thrilling to come home for lunch and watch the diggers
       dig up the ground.
"What's gonna be there?" "What are they doing? What are they doing?"

What emerged was a small by our day supermarket,
with that black-glazed stuff that they used to put on the front
which would catch the reflection
and you could look and see your image in it.
That was the style and it became a wonder.
After the war, they had all these dried soups
and frozen foods—so thrilling—
you didn't realize how awful it was. It was so unique!

Then there was Blood's, more of a big home-style marketplace

where you could get practically everything.
In fact, you could get everything.
They had meat, they baked their own beans,
my father loved that place.
He couldn't walk by it without going in there
and picking up something.
Red kidney beans or some sort of cold cuts.
The place smelled of coffee and all kinds of spices.
They had a bakery in the back, a big bakery,
and they baked all kinds of breads and pastries,
which they would distribute throughout the Lynn area.

Stop and Shop was a little corporation;
Blood's was like a European market.
It was a place where you gave the clerk the money
and he stuck in a pneumatic tube
and sent it to a central cashier—
that kind of Old-World thing.

I liked the bakeries with their smells
and I liked Blood's with its smells
and the incredible variety.
And then there were these Kennedy's stores
with their butter and cheese.
I used to love to watch them cut butter out of a big tub.
You had to line up for your pound of butter.

The Three of Us

Jeanette Carter   Flora Epps   Doris Harewood

THE THREE OF US

We used to go to the dances in Boston, the three of us, and then there was a whole gang of us. Nobody had cars in those days.

We'd go to the dances in Boston, get the last bus home, 2:30 bus, from Revere, walk, 'cause I lived on Shepard St., she lived on Summer Circle, she lived on Alley St. We'd walk down to say Summer St., and we'd all split and we'd go our separate way and never think about it.

Nobody bothered you. Would no body bother you. And to think you're carrying your bag in your hand, swinging your bag.

SUMMER CIRCLE

1

My mother was from North Carolina and my father was from Virginia and they came here because of jobs. He got a job in a bank, at the Social Security downtown. No not Social Security, Security National. I don't know if there were any better jobs before that or not. My mother did housework, and like that.

They lived on Summer Circle, moved there about 1918. My father went to school at night. He was a security guard, a big thing. He used to play the piano for the kids on Summer Circle. He was very tall and he was well-respected.

2

I remember Polonsky's barn. It burned down. Down at the end of Summer Circle, down near the railroad tracks. And I had a red hat, a red hat with a great big tussle on the top of it.

My mother used to make me wear it and I hated that hat and then the day after Polonsky's barn was burned down, it was still burning but the fire was put out, and I ran out and my mother said,

"Don't go down that street," and I went down the street anyhow. I ran down the bottom and I lost my hat. I was so happy. I didn't even care.

And I'm comin' out of the barn and and I looked up and here was two hosses and they were on fire. God, and those two hosses chased me out and up the street and that's when I lost my hat. I ran up the street and I ran in the house screaming and hollering from fear: "Help me! Help Me! They're gonna kill me!" And I think I lost my hat then. I was glad.

And they shot the hosses. Oh, it was so awful. Yeah, when the hosses were on fire, they shot the hosses. It was a terrible experience. I've never seen anything like it right up until this day, and I'm glad of it.

3

Oh yes, the Kellys, oh God. They were a large family and they would beat you to death if you looked at them sideways. Oh God, the day I had those high heels on, I'll never forget.

I had on some high-heeled shoes and I had them all tied around my ankles with strings so they would stay on and I was sittin' down on, on the curbstone in front of Lucy's house, and Nelly come out and she gave me such a hard whack and I tried to run up after her and I couldn't catch up with my high heels on. So I said, "I'm gonna get you later!"

And then my mother told me, "Go out and sweep the gutter! Go out and sweep the gutter. Never mind." So I went out and I swept up the gutter and I looked up and there was Nelly. I says, "I've got you now sister!" Yeah, I ran across the street and I hit her on the back of her head with that dustpan and I flew home.

4

I got hit by a car on the corner—where Himmel's Drugstore was—I got hit by a GE truck.
They said that they'd blackball my father if we did, so my mother didn't sue.
They gave my mother a hundred dollars or something.
A hundred dollars—that was it—that wasn't much money.

That GE did a lot of dirty things—a lot of dirty things. My father didn't work for GE. He worked for the bank. They said they would blackball him, at the bank, at all banks, at all jobs, everywhere, anytime, if he sued. That's right.

I was in first grade when I got hit and I came home and I said, "I'm not gonna tell my mother." She'd say I had no business to be hit by a car, and I didn't tell her I got hit, and the pain in my stomach got so bad, the next day my mother says to me, "Girl, what happened to you?" "Nothin' Ma." And the guy that hit me came knocking at the door and said, "How is your little girl?" My mother says, "Why do you want to know?" "I hit her yesterday with my truck…"

So she took me up to the doctor and I had on this little print dress with bloomers to match, so she took me up to the doctor's and told me, "You go in the room, you sit on the table and you take your clothes off." "Take my clothes off? No way!" Well, they fought with me 'til finally I took off my clothes. They had me on my stomach. And they said I had internal damage. And when I came back, and they said, "What did the doctor do?" "Nothin'." I wouldn't tell 'em I had to take off my clothes and my bloomers too. I thought that was terrible.

—Jeanette Carter

MY MOTHER

1

For my mother, Barbados was always home. Everybody else had a picture of President Roosevelt in their house; we had the Queen of England. "That's my queen." My house was open to everybody. My mother always had pots on the stove cooking: black-eyed peas, red gravy.

What made me so mad about her, my mother never used a cookbook. I have five cookbooks, I have a Kitchen-Aide mixer, I got a blender, electric knives. My mother had none of those things and she was the world's best cook. I said, "Mom, how do you do this? How do you do that?" "Oh, a little bit of this, a little bit of that until it feels just right."

2

I remember one time, my mother had a wart on the back of her neck. She went downstairs, pulled some hair off the tail of a horse, wrapped it around the wart and it fell off.

They used to say they never went to doctors. Her grandmother raised my mother and one time she had something on her skin. Her grandmother went into the yard, I think it was aloe, which they use today, I guess it grew wild over there, I don't know, and she'd get it out and get a piece, break it, it's got a couple strings to it, and you rub it on and whatever was on there would go away.

My mother always said about going to visit someone in the West Indies, and she had on white silk stockings, my mother and her white silk stockings, and a dog. These people had a dog and she was going up to see her, and the dog, no line, came up to her and bit her, and I'm afraid of dogs to this day, and he grabbed her and he bit her! Anybody else would probably have ah, hydrophobia, or whatever they get, but my grandmother went out into the yard and got something-or-other, I don't know, and put it on the foot. My mother still, you can see the marks on her leg.

What it was I don't know, but they do understand a lot of these preserves and they use them and you know, they work. I had a rash on my hand up here… My mother mixed something all up and she put it on and the rash went away.

3

And you know what she used to tell, another funny thing she used to tell me, this is in Prohibition days. Some little old Italian lady, and my mother she didn't know from nothin', and they asked to put something in, it was my brother, I don't think I was born then, put something in the baby's carriage and bring it down someplace. Where it was, my mother didn't know. Well, she had to bring this package and deliver it someplace. My mother… a bootlegger! I couldn't ride a bike and she was ah, you know, a bootlegger! And she took such a chance. "What if you got caught?" I'd ask her. "I didn't know," she'd say.

—Doris Harewood

PREJUDICE AT WORK

1

My father's people came from Virginia. My mother came from Nova Scotia. My grandmother came from Nova Scotia. My grandfather came from the St. Thomas Islands and he came up on a boat all the way to Nova Scotia and that's how he met her. My father's people lived in Woburn and when my mother married into it, he lived in Woburn at that time, and then they came to Lynn 'cause they thought Lynn was the big city. 1924 maybe.

My father worked at the GE forever. He retired from the GE. He's dead now. He retired from the GE. He was in the foundry. They were all in the foundry. It was a hot, dirty, noisy place. My father was a crane operator and I remember one time he told me, "There is prejudice here at work."

2

When I grew up in high school, there were five Black kids in my class—1946.

In '45, there was three. In '47, what? Two? I didn't think about it at all. I was just part of that group. We didn't think about Blacks. Only, my brother Sonny used to beat up everybody. He'd beat 'em up no matter what color they were, he'd beat 'em up.

I took an exam down at GE—1946. I was not the brightest and not the stupidest. I took the exam down there. I didn't get it. I couldn't get into GE and my father worked there. I couldn't get a job period!

You'd get out of high school and they'd have all the jobs. I was as smart as they were. When you got out of high school you worked at the shoe shops, you went to the laundry, babysat. That's about all you could do. Housework. Yeah, housework.

Then the factories started opening up after the war. We could not get a job. And people said, "You're up north. What do you mean you can't get a job? You're up north." I mean, these people are so blind.

I got a job in Boston, at the John Hancock. You see all trucks around and all the people working and everything, you know. It was really something.

3

> Then there was this girl I knew,
> why she worked at the 5 and 10
> 'cause she could pass for white.
> That's why she got a job there.
> Then somebody told the people she worked for
> that she was Black
> and she was fired.
> Woolworth's… downtown.

—Flora Epps

In My Mother's Kitchen

> Those kidneys
> kidneys and rice
> and gravy
> Lima beans and rice
> lima beans and rice
> That's all she ever cooked
> Liver
> liver and bacon
> and onions
> Oh I loved that
> I make it to this day

and of course
that potato soup
which is now I love it
which is potato and water
and onions
and any kind of meat
you had left over
like a hambone
and a lot of fish
'cause fish was cheap

Boys would go fishing   Men too

—Flora Epps

BRICKYARD PENTECOSTALS

1

The Pentecostals, they were small. They were a storefront; they used to be on Blossom St. The church was on several little storefronts in the area of the Brickyard. It originated on Charles St. years and years ago, I remember their saying to us, on Charles St. Then it was, remember the pizza place on Summer St. near Vine, it used to be there. And then it was above the chicken store there on Blossom St. Singer's Chicken, it was upstairs. And then I don't know where the last place was where they went from before they came to Commercial St.

Yeah, I used to love to hear them sing, oh man. Mrs. Savory used to bang that piano. She was a heavy lady and she really used to bang that piano. Alma Savory, she's my mother's, when my mother got married, she was her flower girl. She was a hairdresser; she still is.

And then this little group of people, they're amazing, they were only about… I don't know if there were twenty members in the church, those people got together and they tithed their salaries and they built a little church on Commercial St. It's still there. They built that church. I don't think there were more than twenty people. But they got together, and, it can be done… none of them were fabulously rich or anything, you know. They all had their own homes and their families to raise, but they were determined they were gonna have a church. And they got together and they have their church.

Then they had another group of Pentecostals—Mr. Greenwich. He was from Cambridge, and he had a storefront. There were a lot of little groups you know. They had a church on Summer Circle right where the Kellys lived. Right in the middle of Summer Circle, in a house there. Then he had one on Shepard St., and then on Summer St. where Kushner's was.

He used to preach on a corner. He didn't have a church. He used to preach on a corner, the corner of Summer Circle and Summer St. He was a short man, a husky guy, glasses, slightly bald. He wore a little black suit with a white shirt and a black tie. I think he moved from the different houses 'cause he couldn't afford the rent. My mother's church, they always had a storefront and paying members.

—Doris Harewood

No Idea

1

When it all started changing?   I don' know
In the early 60s   did it start changing in the early 60s?
You had an inflow of new people
that didn't help matters any   no it didn't
and now that I think about it, we didn't do much to help them either
When I think about it   help the people?   Yeah, we didn't do anything
I think it's as much our fault as theirs   'cause they were in there
They didn't know any better and we didn't do anything
No it's true   I often think about that   I think we used to laugh at it
Now when I think about it—how cruel it was
We did nothin' to ah, to make their transition from
wherever they came from any easier
Lotta people from the South   they lived in
well, compared to what they had…

2

I remember one lady from the South
she said a lot of times she saw her husband
he was working in the fields or something
and I think the Ku Klux Klan came
and took him away
and that was it
She never saw him again
That was, that was in like…
the 40s?… No, no the 50s
She had a couple of kids
She came up here
She never knew what happened to him
She was runnin' away from there

3

She was looking for an apartment on Lawrence St.
and the man slammed the door in her face
This is up north, you know, quotation marks
She told me that
She came up to me, out of breath
and I said, "What's the matter with you?"
She said she looked at this apartment
there was an ad in the paper or whatever
so she got up early
she had two kids at the time
and the man slammed the door
right in her face

So we wrote a letter. It was published in the *Item*, about you know,

> Here we are. We're born here, went to school here, work here you know, and we go to get an apartment, and our money, which is the same color as everybody else's money, but our faces are a different color, and the man slams a door in her face.

And at that time, remember, Eddie had fought in Viet Nam, he'd gone to Viet Nam, this friend of mine, and um, we threw that in there too.

4

It was not easy to get an apartment. You were more or less in one little area. That's where you were. It's just lately that we've started to spread out. I don't know what they think is gonna happen if we spread out. "There goes the neighborhood." Like that's gonna happen.

I mean there's good and bad in all. There's white people that I don't want to live beside. And there are Black people I don't want to live beside. So don't think that all Blacks, they're this and they're that. All whites are they're this and they're that.

5

people don't know what's it like for that to happen
they have no idea
they think they must be makin' that up
they have no idea

she had no idea
I'm the first person she has been that close to
yeah, you know America
you know she had no idea

take the girl in the office where I worked
she had no idea
she used to work in a five and ten
and then I explained to her
we had to work in shoe factories
we couldn't get in the five and ten
she had no idea

THE THREE OF US TALK ABOUT URBAN RENEWAL

1

"My house is where the tech is now"
"My house too"

2

"My father was still livin' when it started
He died in '67
In between that time they sent letters to everybody
who they were taking their home and
they sent us an offer and
you got more money if you bought a house immediately and
they would give you the extra money so
I bought a house immediately!
I got a house
It was the smartest thing I ever did"

3

"Mayor Marino
they didn't want to move
His mother used to wash clothes every day
She'd scrub clothes
eight kids
eight or nine kids?
and that clothesline
would be spar-kel-ling
just sparkling
She'd have clothes up there
on that line
every single day

and he didn't want to move away from down there
and he raised Cain when they came through with the urban renewal"

4

"I would have stayed where I was"

Ruth Tansey

Ruth Tansey's Brickyard

1

I love the Brickyard. There was nothing like it. I was born at the Lynn Hospital, May 27, 1927, and my mum and dad took me home to Dowling Terrace, and that's where my life began, as part of, in the Brickyard, and ah, I just love the Brickyard.

I'm a person that likes to socialize with people, and people were just like that in the Brickyard. Everybody took care of everybody. Didn't matter what color you were, what nationality. Nothin'. Religion? We were just all good friends. If someone was havin' a baby, the mothers that lived in the Terrace would go over and help out the family.

2

When I first moved there, there used to be a fence between Dowling Terrace and Westminster Terrace and the kids one year tore down the fence, and had a bonfire, but it was the best thing they did because it made the street wider and cars could get through. Cars were starting to get popular then.

There's nothing like memories. When you're older, like I am now, and not getting out as much as you used to, it's so wonderful to have these memories, 'cause you think back, and they fill you with joy, yeah, fill you with a lot of joy.

3

My mother played the accordion and the piano and my brother was musical also, so we would get out there in the Terrace and have dances and it was fabulous. My mother always taught every kid who was in the neighborhood how to dance. If they couldn't dance, she would just dance with them and show them.

My mother and dad were born here, but my great grandmother and grandfather were Irish and they came from Ireland, Galway Bay area, and my Italian grandmother left her husband. He was no good. So she says, "I'm going to America," and she had my Uncle Tony at the time, and she came here. Took guts. She's a great lady. We used to have a lot of fun with her.

My Irish grandmother was very stoic, but we had a lot of fun with her too. My Italian grandmother was just like a kid, liked to have a good time. But my Irish grandmother would take my Italian grandmother Maria into the bathroom—try to get her to smoke. So my grandmother never smoked and she puffed a cigarette and choked: "You know I don't like it." And she tried to get her to drink. Grandma didn't like that neither.

HOME COOKING

1

My father was a chef, the head chef at Huntt's in the Square. That's where everybody would go. That was the place to go to eat something. You'd go there.

My dad taught us how to cook. On Sundays. we'd all be in the kitchen with him, washing and peelin' the vegetables, and he taught us how to trim the meats, and my mother, he taught her how to bone everything, and he'd use the bones for the soups, and that's how I got to be interested in cooking.

And then, before I was married, when I started to pay board, I said to my dad, my dad wouldn't allow Italian food in the house, Irish you know, he just didn't want it in the house, so I said, "I'm workin' now and I'm paying board. Would it be all right dad if I could start cookin' Italian food?" And who do you think ate it? My father. He loved it. And it was good, so we had a balance of Irish and Italian.

2

My Grandmother King used to board Irish people, the relatives, they came to Lynn from the old country. Every Sunday, we had to go to Grandma King's house for dinner. This was an obligation and we had to go. And my dad used to say, "You sit in your chairs and I don't want to hear a word out of your mouth. Just be quiet." And my other cousins would raise holy hell.

Whenever there was a bridal shower or something important, my dad and my mother and the children would cook everything and serve it. And one day, my aunt was leaving with her family and she said as she left, "Let the guineas clean up afterwards," and my mother heard it, and she said, "We'll never cook for you people again, and don't you ever talk that way about my nationality to my children or anybody."

J.B. Blood's

I was a cashier at J.B. Blood's

On the days I wasn't busy
I would go across the building
the Blood Building
and ah
either pack eggs
or slice cheese
and then wrap 'em up
price 'em out
and cold cuts and things
like that
tea and coffee

bag 'em

and when we used to go
by the deli counter
there was always a big tub
of peanut butter
Dip your finger in it
and eat it!

Heh heh
It was delicious

St. Mary's

When my husband died, I sold my home and I came here to St. Mary's. They treat me wonderful in here. There's only a few of us from the Brickyard left. I've lived here about 22 years. It was where I was brought up. I wanted to come back here 'cause I knew the church and I loved St. Mary's.

We used to have May processions every summer and we'd go into the Commons and walk all around, up to the Greek church and come around back to St. Mary's. We'd gather at the armory and we'd have a grand march. They don't do those things any more. And it was fabulous. The monsignor would go first and then the nuns and then the priests and then us. And it was just... my mother used to take all the kids to that because their parents didn't want to go, so the kids would go with mum and ah, we just had a lot of fun.

And then St. Francis Church, that's where my mother and my auntie went, they would have their fiesta time and the big procession with the blessed Mother and the dollar bills and ten-dollar bills hangin' on her and we used to love that 'cause we'd get into that procession too. Sorry I don't have pictures. I just didn't feel up to gettin' them. OK?

My faith is very important. It's number one. My husband came in one day, he said, "You love Christ more than me." "He's number one, then you." My faith is really important. I love my ministry here because you know I love to gab. And I enjoy the people that I went to and I became so close to them. They became like a family. I gave communion in church and I brought communion to people who couldn't get out. And I just loved it. People would just, well I knew so many of them. When I first moved here, it was filled with St. Mary's, the Brickyarders.

Delores Jackson

DELORES JACKSON'S BRICKYARD

The Brickyard had a few reunions, but I never went to them. I knew there was a Brickyard, but I wasn't all involved or anything.

The boundaries were Blossom St., some people said Shepard. As far as even going down to Commercial, they say "No no, you're not the Brickyard." The Brickyard basically stopped at Shepard St. That's what they were sayin'. For me, it would have been from Blossom St. to Commercial. And parts back there by Hood Milk. That's what I would say.

My mother was born on West St. in 1901. She was actually born in the house of Jan Matzeliger, the man who invented the shoe lasting machine. And she lived there, I know that she lived there for about eight years. After that, they probably rented homes that her father, my grandfather rented, in here, I don't know what streets, but I know he bought the house on Prospect St. in 1922. I was raised in that house. That's the only house I ever lived in until urban renewal came. Told us we all had to go!

54 PROSPECT STREET

1

When my grandfather went to buy the house (I wasn't born yet), but the lady who sold it to him, she sold it to him, the neighbors didn't know that he was a Black man buying this house, you'd run into that, but she sold it. Once it was sold there was nothing they could do about it. They weren't too happy I guess about the fact it was a Black person. But it was a decent family that was moving into the house. And I was fine with the neighbors. I grew up and went to school with the kids and I was fine.

2

Our house had fruit trees. We had pear trees, we had a peach tree and a grapevine in the backyard. They used to make, my grandmother used to make jelly and take the pears and preserve the pears, you know, put 'em in jars and stuff like that.

My house was 54, and then there was another house, 56, and then there was a big open field. I guess years ago, there was housing that was torn down, but there just was a field.

By the time I got married, it was just my mother and my grandmother. In my mind, I planned on getting an apartment across the street so I could be close by. But we wound up staying in the house. The house was what? Three bedrooms, you know. It was a seven-room house so we stayed in the house. And actually I had my first, well, both kids were born there. My grandma died in '64, so we still stayed there.

3

We stayed until renewal came and told us we all had to go. They told us they were going to revitalize the city of Lynn. It wasn't like you had to get out immediately. In fact, some of the people stayed. Some of the people had really done their houses over nice, and they still wanted to give you small money for it, so some people stayed longer to fight to get a couple more thousand dollars, you know, towards it.

Our house was an older house; you had to patch it up. The plumbing was starting to go. The heat, the pipes underneath, you had to make sure in the wintertime they didn't freeze. My husband went underneath and wrapped the pipes up. Eventually we would have moved, but on our own time, you know what I mean?

4

Now when we went looking for housing, this is to buy another house, and bein' in the post office, we knew the city. If you say a street, we could tell you where it was, and most of the realtors, they wanted to put you in the predominantly Black areas. Certain streets, there's more Black people. In fact, the house we got was not. When we were lookin', we went to look at a house in Salem, and the people who were living in that house, their daughter was sellin' a house in Lynn. And so we came to the house in Lynn, that the realtors in Lynn, they never bothered showin' us. It was a regular house, a cottage, and we were very happy there until we just downsized a few years ago.

Church

We went to St. Stephen's Episcopal Church, that's at the corner of Blossom and South Common. We're still members of that church, but also, what we used to do as kids, we used to spend all day in church. We would go to St. Stephen's in the morning, and then we would go to the Bethlehem Pentecostal Church in the afternoon for Sunday School, and we also went to the Gregg House, which is Congregational.

That church they built up, the Pentecostal Church. They started up over the chicken store on Blossom St., and then from there they went to Commercial St. And they built a church and now they're down on Light St. Bethlehem Temple... 'cause we always call it by the name of the ministers—Bethlehem Temple Pentecostal Church. There was about five families that built that church and of course they came from the islands. There was five families that basically got that church goin'. Matter of fact, one of the ladies, she just passed away this week. In fact, you mentioned her. Doris Harewood. She passed away this week. Her mother and father and four other families started that church. Years ago... yup.

Getting Work

My grandfather was very worldly. He loved to talk politics and everything. But of course, he was a Black man so he was just gonna get the menial jobs.

When I was in high school, I was a good student, I'll pat myself on the back, but they say there were part-time jobs, and after a while I told the teacher, "Don't send me for those jobs, 'cause they don't want me. As soon as they see me, they don't want me there." It was true. I did get a couple of part-time jobs. I worked in a bakery on Summer St. after school, the New York Model Bakery. I also worked part time at the shoe factory in the office. And I had to make a big decision, was I goin' to stay at the office, they did offer me permanent work, or was I going to go into Boston?

Then when I got out of high school, there were smart Black girls, young ladies, but "You're not gonna get a job in Lynn." That's all there was to it. Then one friend, she actually put her foot on the steps of the City Hall to go into City Hall to see about a job, in fact even when I went over for a job—they come out: "Oh no, that job's been taken. You don't even need to come into the building." So I went into Boston, an insurance company. I worked there.

RECOGNITION

1

My mother worked with Abner Darby and Virginia Barton and Allen Mitchell and they went up to the state house to see about getting recognition for Jan Matzeliger. And when they start getting recognition for him, that's when they even got the stamp, the postal stamp that was issued, what, 1991.

2

Then also the bridge they dedicated
that's up…
I got a picture of that
the bridge…
that's right here
It's not there where the house was
'cause that's all gone
that whole area is gone
but that's up East Lynn
mmhmm, Green St. bridge
mmhm, and they had that
they dedicated that

The plaque is there
on the bridge now
Somebody had marked on it
you know how they do vandalism
that was… ah, and also
she went up to the cemetery
They had a service at the cemetery
I have a picture of it… yeah

They were all at the cemetery
at his gravesite

3

Growing up, I didn't know my mother lived in that house. In fact, by that time the house was torn down. But it was around the corner. Anytime you walked in the area, you walked right by it. But I wasn't aware of it at that time, no. And of course, we weren't taught this in school. Then later on, she got involved, I really can't tell you how. I learned about Jan Matzeliger through my mother. We weren't taught this in school.

4

My mom was always very active. She died when she was 95. When she was about 90, she got sick and went into rehab, and we went to see her there and she was just layin' up there. I'm thinking, "What's goin' on?" This is not this woman, you know. And at that time, I told her they were workin' on the stamp. Well, that was the medicine she needed! Next thing you know she was up and out of that rehab and back out on her two feet and working on it.

So yeah, she was very happy about the recognition and everything. And then the First Day of Issue for the stamp, she was in it, she had a speech to make. That was actually in a museum. We were upstairs. They did it upstairs near the lasting machine and the Matzeliger exhibit. They had representation from Washington D.C.

Oh yeah, she participated, on everything, she spoke, you see pictures of her in the paper. She's talking to, um the channel, from Channel 5, you know the television person that'll come. She's talkin' to him, she's very relaxed, she never got nervous. And she's tellin' him about her story. And the legacy of all this is that Matzeliger gets recognition, credit for inventing the lasting machine, and my mother gets credit for her part in bringing that about.

Gordon Laro

MY PEOPLE

My father was born in 1904, 1906, somewhere in that neighborhood.
He came to Lynn from Worcester when he was four.
He went to school with Patsy Caggiano and Primo Lombardi and those guys.
They all went to the Washington School and the Shepard School.

My father worked at Goddard Brothers for 27 years.
They finally went out of business in the early 50s
and left everybody to fend for themselves.
He was the night watchman, the elevator operator and the shipper.

And while he was working there, he met my mother.
My mother was from New Glasgow, Nova Scotia.
I was born in 1939, in the house, on Summer Circle, 46,
next to the last house on the street, across from the Growitzs.

THE CURRENT

summertime we used to go down the gas wharf and go swimmin'
some of the guys used to get a raft
go out on the current that's down there
wind up in the middle of the harbor

then you're in trouble
we had poles but once you get out so far
then the poles are no good
especially if the tide was in

it was a current that come out from the gas company
we called it the current but it was just a thing
where all the stuff come out
it was water that just came right out
and had a nice current to it

you put a raft in there
it take you way on out in the middle of the harbor

it was just like hittin' a stream
some guys would go out and they swim back
leave the raft out there
a few guys went out a few times
they didn't know how to swim
so they had to get rescued

the current's still there
you go down right across the street on Blossom St.
the continuation of Blossom St.
all the way down to where the boat comes in
and there's a ramp there where you drive down
and put your boat in the water
right over to the right you'll see a little thing
where the water's comin' out
and that's where we use' ta put rafts in

CORNER PECKING ORDER

You never got to learn nothin'
because you got on the corner with the older guys
and they'd give ya a boot in the butt and tell ya to keep steppin'.
Nobody wanted you to learn too fast.
You couldn't hang on the corner with the big boys
'cause the big boys don't want none of the younger guys around.

If I was twelve and the guy was sixteen
I couldn't hang around on the corner wid him
'cause they all had their own little group that they were hanging with
and there'd be a group here with guys maybe sixteen or seventeen
and here'd be a group of guys in their twenties
and these guys were on one side
and those guys were on the other side.

If we tried to get on the corner,
hang around, see what everybody's sayin',
they kick you in your [hmmph]… tail
and tell ya to keep on steppin'.

So ya never learned nothin' from nobody in those days.
If you wanted to learn, you had to experience your own thing
and when you got old enough,
you could hang on the corner with the rest of the guys.

RATS

Then ya had rats   oooh   I mean rats
these were rats
I never seen rats that big anywhere
with the tail, a good two feet long
or maybe better
and if they stretched out   hoo
they were bigger than cats
You couldn't use a cat for those rats

You had a grain house right across the railroad tracks on Alley St.
and they use' ta go over there and fill up
There was a combination of wharf rats that came in from—
well, the water wasn't that far away

They came into the land lookin' for food
They hit the grain house and they happen to stay around there
so I guess they went on patrols every night
and they hit all the houses in the neighborhood

It was always—
everybody had rats in that neighborhood
Everybody I talk to that lived in that neighborhood
even Alley St.
told me about these rats that we used to have around here

They were there alright
I'm talkin' about—inside
not outside—inside
My mother killed two or three of them when I was a kid
That was when I lived on 46
'cause we were closer to the railroad tracks
And she killed
I woke up one mornin' and she killed one—
his tail was that fat!
easily an inch around
He was a big one
and she hit him with a poker

She got up every mornin' like about five
to stir the ashes in the fire and get the heat goin'
so she had a poker in her hand and she heard a noise
all this rumblin' and stuff

and I came out and she had just killed a rat
Like I said it was just like that
so I carried it out and threw it out outside in the barrel

It wasn't like people were getting bitten
but they were in the houses

PIGEONS

The guy next door was raisin' rabbits
and my father had pigeons. Homing pigeons.
And a guy across, Rudy Growitz,
I think he got the idea from my father about homing pigeons
and then he got into it
and he went even further that my father
because he had more money to invest.
He used to take his pigeons all the way down to Virginia
and places like that and then let them fly back.

My father had two hundred pigeons at one time.
He kept them in the backyard at 46.
We had a garage and up top he built a coop
and he use' ta keep 'em up there.
Then next door was Morris Crawford and he had pigeons too.
He had a little coop over a shed.
He and my old man had them together.

URBAN BLIGHT

1

In '51, '52, in that area, we moved from 46 to 34 Summer Circle.
There was more room. We were getting' bigger
and the house there wasn't big enough for all of us.
In those days people moved either because they needed more room
or where they were livin' was getting too shabby to take care of.

2

The landlords there, they didn't like to spend any money.
They liked to milk 'em dry and go from there.
On Summer Circle, they never took care of their houses.
And they let a lot of people in there which were bad for the street,
ruined the street, 'cause there used to be trees all up and down Summer Circle.
The people that they allowed to move there, that came from out of state,
they're the ones that did the houses in.
But like I say, it goes back,
the landlords didn't want to take care of the houses.
All they wanted was the steady income of the money.
And that's what really ruined those houses. People were gettin' greedy.

The same landlords that owned a lot of that property that went downhill,
they were pushin' the people into all their properties.
If you got burned out of one house they'd move you into another house,
another one of their properties.
They were all cousins.
They'd try to keep them all in one house,
try to put 'em all on one block and you get a whole block built up.
So instead of having empty spaces, you got a whole block built up.

3

Summer Circle was either getting burnt out or the buildings were just being shut up.

Like across the street from me was a big block, I think it was a nine-family house and it was all boarded up. They had a fire in one part of it and it might have cost a few… well in those days maybe ten thousand dollars woulda done the whole house over, made it look good. But they got all they wanted out of it and they let it go.

So that went, and the same thing on that other block and then on two or three more blocks. So, they started lettin' these things go and after a while they became eyesores and the street starts lookin' bad. You might have three or four houses on the street that look good, but then you have ten that don't look good. So after a while there was hardly anybody livin' there.

They had all moved off and there was two blocks that always had people in 'em and as you came down Summer Circle then all of a sudden there was nobody livin' there. By that time, my mother had moved off the street. I was still livin' there, but I was very seldom home. My brother Frankie was down there 'til the end.

BRICKYARD CORNER STORES

1

Mrs. Bregan's was next door to my grandmother's house.
I went there a few times, but they didn't have that much.
Bregan's was a variety store, but it wasn't that big of a variety store.
Everytime you went in there, the shelves were mostly empty.
If they run out of somethin', it took 'em awhile to replace it.

If you wanted variety, you'd have to go to Levine's on Blossom.
He had a bigger store and he had more of it.
He was always getting a fresh shipment in.
In his store you could get anything you wanted
and my mother used to have a bill with Izzy.

He was makin' more money, and he cuffed.
Everybody used to run a bill and then you'd go in there,
my mother used to send us over on my father's payday with the money,
and you'd bring back the slip and give it to her you know.
Then you could start a new one.

Now down on the other corner, on the corner of Alley and Blossom was
    Jack's.
Now Jack had most of the people on Alley St. that used to cuff with him.
And Harbor, and that section. He had a cuff for those people,
but down there we had to pay cash.

2

Now there's a store where Jack's used to be.
I was in there yesterday.
Every Sunday, I go down and get my paper.
And all the guys, they're older than me,
was one guy, he got there early yesterday,
I didn't get to see him,
and was a couple of guys,
maybe a year or two older than me
that I did hang around with from Shepard St.
that come down,
one from Blossom going up further towards the Commons,
he hangs out there, Carrodi, then Eddie King—he's from Shepard.
Now they're there on Sundays, usually.
Rudy's usually there every Sunday, but he went to St. Louis

so he won't be in 'til probably next week.
Then we got Frank Lombardi, or Hot Dog as they call him,
Sam's brother. Sam was there yesterday too.
They're mostly all Italians.
Then the Pasquale twins, Joe and Angelo.
They're from Summer Circle. They hang out down there.
They go to church at St. Francis and after church they come down for coffee
and we all sit around and talk about different things that're goin' on.
It's a little session that we have every week.
And you get to see guys you haven't seen.
Like if you miss a few weeks and you go down there,
sooner or later someone's going to find you.
Like, ah, Farese came down there one day.
He was born above Bregan's store, and later on he moved to Blossom St.
He's livin' down in Florida and he came back—
first place he headed for was that store—
'cause he knows all of us hang around there.
So he come back lookin' to see who's around.
A few of the guys are his age,
so they're hangin' around, jivin', shootin' the bull.

3

I was talkin' to one guy, he's a painter,
I worked with him when I was in the GE,
and he came from, I think he was raised on Alley St.,
and he was talking about when he was in the CCC camps.
So was Frank Lombardi.
He was in the CCC camps, he was talkin' about it.
What they had to do and all that.
But Pickle, the painter,
he liked it because he says he grew about six inches in one year.
He says, all the food you wanted to eat, ice cream he says.
You know it was real funny listening to him talk.
You know he says one place he was at, it had to be close by,
oh I think it was building Breakheart,
he says they were throwing out all kinds of pork chops, so he got some paper,
    wrapped 'em up and he says he used to take them home every night.
His mother told him, "Don't ever leave that place."

4

The store closes at 12:00 and the older guys get there from 11:00 to 12:00.
Most of the guys, he holds their papers for them.
In the warm weather, they stand on the corner and talk.
They talk about Megabucks they just missed or reminisce about the old days
shoot the breeze   see who's running at Suffolk that day
and then they go down to the Italian Club on Harbor St., have a few drinks,
or they go down The 50 Club, 'cause that was an old hangout for 'em.

5

I bring my little grandson around with me all the time.
He goes down to the corner store with me and all that.
He loves it down there.
Sunday mornings he's gettin' dressed
ready to go with me.

There's a guy who lives across the street
owns a house.
He's got a German Shepherd
and my grandson loves that dog
so I take him over
and let him play with him for a while.
Nice dog.

Eleanor Fisher

Eleanor Fisher's Brickyard

I never heard of the name Brickyard until ten years ago.

My grandparents, my mother's parents came from Odessa, Russia. My mother came over when she was five or six years old, and my grandfather had a tinsmith's shop right on Summer St. I remember the shop. It was green outside and it was like one room, and he had stoves in there. And he would repair stoves and anything that would come along he would repair that had to do with tin.

My house was on Commercial St., one block up from the corner of Commercial and Neptune. My grandparents were Orthodox Jews. They lived upstairs from us, it was a two-family house, and my father worked and my mother worked and my grandparents took care of me.

And I remember one sad thing—when my folks were trying to sell the house, they were living in Revere at that time, and I went back to try to get a table out of the attic, a huge round oak table you know, and my doll carriage from when I was a little girl, and the house was all vandalized. I felt just terrible; it made such an impression.

And then when I went back and saw the house had been torn down; it was an empty lot. And I heard two stories about what happened to the house. One was that it sold and the other story I heard was they couldn't sell it and the city took it over. So I don't know which is the truth.

The Firehouse on Commercial Street

The fire station was directly across the street from my house and it was a very important nucleus of the neighborhood. People felt safe because they knew it was there. And they were like the neighborhood policemen. They knew all the kids and the firemen didn't get changed. It was a place you could count on; they knew the kids, they knew who was acting out, they would talk to them, they would play with them.

I could go over, if my mother or father wasn't home, I could go over and sit on the bench in front of the firehouse and know I would be all right. Or if I was sitting on my front steps, waiting for the kids or something, they would always say, "Hi Eleanor. What's happening? How are you?" And sometimes I had friends over from other neighborhoods and I could be a big shot and bring them into the fire station and they would call me by name.

And every night my father played pinochle with them and that was the thing. He'd have dinner and go across the street. My dad played horseshoes at the firehouse. They had big horseshoe tournaments there; they played behind the firehouse.

And in 1949, I remember clearly, they got their first television and I went over and I watched Ed Sullivan and Milton Berle and Mickey Mouse. I always felt welcome and right in back of where the engines were, they had the kitchen, and I remember smelling what they were cooking in the big pots. It was a very welcoming place and it was the safest place to be.

DATING RULES

The Jewish kids just knew you must not date a Gentile

You could have Gentile friends
but no Gentile boy friends or girl friends
That was forbidden and you knew that

Sex   I remember when I was dating
I got a hickey on my neck
and my mother looked at me disgusted
"Do you have to do everything?"
I had discovered necking
I loved to kiss
I had a good time doing that

Sex was a very big taboo
You knew that the boys wanted to touch you
but you never allowed it
You didn't talk about it

Kissing was OK
You could kiss but nice girls wouldn't do any more
and the boys always tried to get you to do more
and it was kind of like a game within the group

You knew in high school
there were some girls who fooled around
You didn't talk to them

THE BALLOON LADY

Have you heard about her?
She may even be still alive.
I saw her two years ago.
She's short; she can't be more than five feet tall,
and she's bald and looks like she shaves.
And she's always around,
always at parades selling balloons.
And so she was called The Balloon Lady,
I remember very very clearly.

She was always an object of scorn, derision.
People didn't feel sorry for her.
By her appearance, she invited negative attention.
That's the only way she was identified—by the balloons
… and the socks and the sneakers.

SUMMER ST.

The individual grocery stores were really nice;
they were like extensions of each family.
You would go to Tobin's and get some eggs,
so Tobin's would know me, and when I would go into Tobin's,
one of them would give me a raw egg
and show me how to eat it.
So I would go into Tobin's and get my mother eggs
and I would get a raw egg.
It was just a thing.

I would go to the butcher store
and I would get something for my mother,
for my grandmother, and I would get
some chopped liver or something,
maybe a taste of raw hamburger,
and it was so different from going to the supermarket.

I was comfortable.
You went to the store, you were known.
I think that was one of the most important things.
Being known and being safe.

Paul Benson

PAUL BENSON'S BRICKYARD

My grandparents were refugees from Russia, Jews, Orthodox Jews.
Somewhere along the line, they came to this country,
settled in the Brickyard on Wheeler St., Wheeler St. Court.
I don't know if people actually called it the Brickyard then,
or where that term comes from. They lived off Summer St.
I don't even know when they came to this country.
It's something they never talked about.

I don't know if people would say, "Gee, I'm from the Brickyard."
They might say, "I live near Summer Street."

Basically, the Common was the great dividing line.
If you lived above the Commons, above North Common St.,
you know, literally it was the opposite side of the track.
South Common was considered what would be the Brickyard,
and there are debates about what streets actually consisted of the Brickyard.

HOW I LEARNED ABOUT THE HOLOCAUST

I went to Lynn Hebrew School on Blossom St.
five days a week, every day after school.
I went there, let's see, in '53, second grade,
and I completed six years there
and then on Saturday, we were supposed to go to Shabbat services.
I can't remember anything in Hebrew to this day.

There were many synagogues in that area.
Way back you had a synagogue on Church St.
We went to the Shepard St. synagogue.
I had my bar mitzvah there.
It was strictly orthodox, women separated upstairs, men downstairs,
and that's where I went I don't know how many years.
It was a small synagogue.
It wasn't what you call these modern-day temples.

And there was a synagogue on Blossom St.
This was a synagogue where, they would call them greenhorns,
where the greenhorns would go.

The greenhorns were immigrants, Jewish immigrants, post-Holocaust
    survivors.
I had some of my friends, their families were survivors from the Holocaust,
and at a young age I heard some of the stories,
how Mr. Kluger buried himself underground for a couple of years,
and how they were in concentration camps,
and how Si's mother Lotte, she was…
They were all in concentration camps.
She was originally from Berlin, from a sort of upper-crust
Jewish Berlin department-store-owning background.

I grew up with these people. I went to school with their sons
and that was a part of their legacy, the stories and the Holocaust.
And then there were a bunch of other people, some of them,
other than losing everybody in their entire family,
some of the people looked like they went through the grist mill,
where they were just beaten down, beaten over, lucky to be alive,
and there they were, involved in grocery stores, survivors,
and at a young age you would learn,
you would be familiar with the stories of the Holocaust.

CULTURE SHOCK

1

The Brickyard Multi-Service Center on Summer St., a satellite of Lynn Economic Opportunity, was a small storefront. The services they offered were basic: Okay, this is how you get on Welfare, this is what you do here. It was to assist people navigating the system. This was at the height of when the LRA was gearing up to bulldoze everything. I only worked there for the Neighborhood Youth Corps for about a year or so and then I did something else.

2

At one point, I was a tutor in the Washington Community School. The fellow who was coaching the basketball team got a paid job, and not that I'm a great basketball player, but I played the game a little bit, so OK, I volunteer and I will coach the team and by that time the Washington School is primarily Black. So one time we had a game at the Lynn Woods School, which is in Ward 1, which is close to Lynnfield. It's single homes, it's lily-white, it's where the municipal elite lived. Even as an adult, I've had very little dealings with Ward 1.

3

So we go to the Lynn Woods School, we walk in and they have a PA announcement system. It was like walking into a regular college basketball game. They had cheerleaders. My students, the kids from the Washington School, had scruffy, dirty, ripped jackets.

It was an elementary school game. I'm walking around freaked out, the kids from the school were looking around freaked out, and ultimately we played the game and we beat the crap out of them.

I mean, Washington Community School was pretty basic. Our games, it's just come and play ball. We don't have cheerleaders. We don't have announcements. These kids are relatively good ball players. We beat the crap out of them.

EMPTY SPACE

A friend of mine I went to school with,
we graduated in 1964 and he went to Rensselaer Polytech,
and he lived on Shepard St. behind the High Hat Café,
which was on Summer St. He lived on the corner.
Well, he came back from college and his house was destroyed,
bulldozed over, and making a joke he said,
"Yeah, I came back from college and the house was gone
and the whole area looked like the middle of Kansas, one big flat prairie."

A lot of empty space. I do not know the exact scheme
of the Lynn Development Authority, but it was titled
in Martin Anderson's book, *The Federal Bulldozer*.
This is what they did to the Brickyards.
My recollection is that the Brickyard was blighted
and then bulldozed over.

Robert Caro has a book about Robert Moses,
about how in the Bronx Moses bulldozed a vast section of tenements.
I don't know how many buildings or how many blocks.
They just bulldozed that down to build the Cross Bronx Expressway.
The other alternative would be to take a few upper-crust people's houses,
but because they had money, he figured he would destroy
20,000 poor working-class lives instead.

This whole trend, this redevelopment nationwide, the federal bulldozer,
all replicated Robert Moses' approach: poor people have less power
so we can just bulldoze down their area.
What they did to the Brickyard was such a waste. A lot of people got
    short-changed.
If you go down to the Brickyard now, it's so much empty space.

NO SMOKE 2.0

In 1935, my sister's wrist was broken in an accident. She was awarded $25 by an insurance company. When her wrist healed, she used the money to pay for violin lessons in a small studio on Market. St. Her teacher was Vincent Ferrini, poet.

—From a letter to me written by Arthur Polonsky, dated March 28,1988.

1

No Smoke by Vincent Ferrini (1913–2007), published in 1941, is a groundbreaking work of poetry rooted in the city of Lynn during the Great Depression and the New Deal. The collection consists mainly of portraits of Lynn residents Vincent knew from growing up in the Brickyard and from recruiting students for the WPA class he taught. The people Vincent writes about are given fictitious names that serve as titles for the poems, and he also addresses the city, the factories and the Narrow Gauge Railroad. Vincent has great sympathy for the working class and great empathy for all except bosses and capitalists. His poetic vision is expressed in "Waldo Paine," the book's autobiographical poem: "To him, every living thing is a poem."

2

In 2001, at North Shore Community College's annual Celebration of the Poetry of Lynn, the sixtieth anniversary of the publication of *No Smoke* was commemorated. Arnold Trachtman read Vincent's poem "Alfred Jacobs," and later that year, he told me the story of how his distant cousin Benny Alpert, the real Alfred Jacobs, came up with the name for the book.

The poem "Julia Brennan" was the exception to the rule that the title of the poem not be the person's real name. Vincent's presentation of Julia Brennan as a hard-bitten street person is somewhat contradicted by the recollection of Evelyn Lazaris (1926–2012) in her interview conducted on May 26, 1982.

Evelyn taught cosmetology at Lynn Technical Vocational Institute for 25 years and also served as a guidance counselor and summer school principal. In 2003, she was inducted into the Lynn Tech Hall of Fame. She liked to say she went back to the Brickyard every day for work.

Serendipitously, in the spring of 1982, Eleanor took a creative writing course I was teaching nights, and as a result, she introduced me to the other women who were members of her Summer Circle Association. They met monthly to maintain their lasting friendships and reminisce about the Brickyard. Her memories and those of her friends and their spouses formed the core of *Brickyard Stories*.

3

What's clear from these two stories about people profiled in *No Smoke* is that like beauty, individuals are seen through the eyes of their beholders. Interestingly, another even more sympathetic point of view of Julia Brennan is provided by Chick Gecoya in his *Remembrances*. Likewise, Whiskey Pete is perceived more compassionately in *Remembrances* than in the recollection of James McNiff.

Arnold Trachtman

NAMING *NO SMOKE*

plays Beethoven for hours like no one else can
"Albert Jacobs" in *No Smoke*
by Vincent Ferrini [1941]

The great and famous Huntt's restaurant in Central Square
was a refuge for all sorts of people. You could go
and sit there for hours until they closed
and have these long conversations
and nobody would bother you.
Buy a cup of coffee and sit down
and it was the closest thing to a European café around.
Huntt's was famous. Great things happened in Huntt's.

Vincent got the name of his book from Huntt's.
I remember he said he was in there with Benny Alpert
and he said, "Benny, I finished the book. But what will I call it?"
And Benny comes out of Huntt's and they look around,
he looks around, and he says "Why not call it *No Smoke*?

"Albert Jacobs" was the poem that I read at the college.
Vincent gave Benny a pseudonym—Albert Jacobs.
That was Benny Alpert. I knew Benny.
Benny was a distant cousin of mine.

He was an extraordinary musician, a part time musician
because he had to make a living.
He worked at the GE.
He had aspirations to be a composer which were squelched.
But he had all these connections.
He spent a good part of the summer playing piano in night clubs.
He was older. I figured I had a better chance.
I wasn't married. I didn't have kids.
That did it to him. I didn't feel that had to be me.
I always felt somehow I was gonna make it as an artist.

Evelyn Lazaris

JULIA BRENNAN

Who knows where I sleep and who cares?
"Julia Brennan" in *No Smoke*
by Vincent Ferrini [1941]

Where she lived was on the shortcut
from Summer Circle through to Blossom Street.
She lived in the next house by herself
in four rooms with furniture.
She had a cot and a table and no electricity
because I remember when we were kids
we looked through her window
and she had a candle burning.
I don't think she ever read a newspaper
although there were a lot of them in her house.

Julia Brennan walked the streets
always carrying two handbags;
even in summertime
she'd have a hat on and a coat.
It didn't make any difference to her
what the weather was.

Her hair was always unruly
never combed   on the curly side
blondish   but it turned gray
as the years went by.

Every once in a while
she'd be walking down the street
and she'd stop and pull out
something from her bag and she'd eat it
and of course the kids would tease her
but not too much.

You couldn't really talk to her because
she didn't really know how to converse with people.
All she'd ever do was walk up and down the street
picking the barrels.

Every so often
a big black car
would come to her house
and a man would get out
and bring things in to her.
Who the person was
that sent these things
we never knew.
It was speculated there was a sister
who lived in Swampscott that was rich
but we never found out.

And she was found dead
in her four-room apartment one day
and we were all so sad over that.

PART 2:
THE NEW BRICKYARD
AFTER URBAN RENEWAL

THE BRICKYARD AT THE TURN OF THE NEW MILLENNIUM

I spent a lot of weekends at my grandparents' house, where my mom grew up on Dowling Terrace. And of course, my grandmother's rules, whenever I left the house, were don't go up and play on the tracks, and needless to say, you know, Foo! like a magnet to the tracks, right out there.

And, ah... of course I did have to have my initiation into the area. They used to run freight trains near the Terrace, so my initiation was to lay on the gravel on the side of the track as a fifty-car freight train went by and I was about sixty pounds at the time, waiting to get sucked into the wheels, but... I survived.

—Russ Tansey

1

Through the 1990s, I continued to interview Brickyard residents. I didn't go out of my way to find people to interview. I relied on students enrolled in my Composition I writing classes. I recognized Brickyarders from the addresses they wrote on information sheets at the beginning of the semester.

This isn't a big group, but it represents the neighborhood a quarter of a century or so after urban renewal. Theirs is a younger generation that has little knowledge of the history, traditions and legends of the Brickyard covered in this book. They represent a new wave of immigrants to the Brickyard—from the Dominican Republic, from Jamaica, from Russia, from Nigeria. Still, their immigration experiences, the diversity of their countries of origin and the values expressed in their stories connect them directly to the Brickyard before urban renewal.

2

The first three speakers are a trio of young men:

Miguel Soto (1976–   )

I interviewed Miguel on February 5, 1999. Originally from the Dominican Republic, Miguel rented an apartment on Alley St. for a year and a half, and in that time, he was able to absorb and appreciate the neighborhood's way of life.

Gary Abdul (1979–   )

I interviewed Gary on December 14, 1998. Born in Jamaica, Gary told me about life on Vine St. When I asked him about the Brickyard, he said he only knew about the neighborhood from what his teachers at Lynn Tech told him.

Brandy Soto (1976–   )

Brandy told me his Brickyard story one day after class and then agreed to tell it to me again when I could record it, something we did on May 19, 1996. Brandy didn't live in the Brickyard, but his story took place at Lynn Plastics, at the time located on the commercial/industrial block bounded by Alley St. and the Lynnway, between Pleasant St. and Blossom St.

3

The next group of stories all concern Neptune Towers, two twelve-story affordable housing towers opened in 1971. The Towers are the most visually prominent residential outcome of urban renewal, they are the largest housing development in the Brickyard Corridor, and they are open to all ages, not just seniors. In the fifty years that the 339 apartments in the Towers have been rented, thousands of people have lived there.

These Neptune Towers stories show how Towers residents build community into their lives, and at their center are stories of Russian Jews who emigrated to Lynn in the 1990s. A significant number of Jews from Russia had been coming to Lynn since the 1970s, and three of the speakers in this section represent the last wave of those immigrants, this one precipitated by the loosening of restraints by Mikhail Gorbachev in the late 1980s. Bernice Kazis' *Short Stories of a Long Journey: An Oral History of Russian Jewish Resettlement North of Boston* [2002] does an excellent job of placing these stories within the larger sweep of history, and she also points out the importance to these new arrivals of learning English and practicing Judaism.

These are the five speakers who tell their stories about life in Neptune Towers:

Russ Tansey (1950–)

During my interview with his mother Ruth on August 12, 2019, Russ recalled when Neptune Towers opened and compared living there with living in the Brickyard before urban renewal.

Leah Levitin

Leah came to the U.S. from Russia with her five-year-old daughter in September of 1990. She began her studies at Salem State University in January 1992. I interviewed her on August 8, 1994, while she was in a writing class I taught that summer. Although Leah's English was not perfect, I think for her, the interview was a chance to show how far she had come in four years.

Alex Kaplan (1981–)

Alex was in one of my Composition I classes at North Shore Community College when I interviewed him on December 6, 2000, and he told me about his family's emigration from Russia to the U.S.

Dima Kuperman (1983–)

Like Alex, Dima was in a writing class I taught during the fall semester of 2000. During my interview with him on November 22 of that year, he described the Russian community in Neptune Towers and in Lynn. He told me about antisemitism in the Ukraine, made clear the role of the car in his life, and explained what it was like for him to live in Neptune Towers.

Kenechukwu (Kenneth) Ofonagoro (1961–)

I interviewed Ken on May 2, 2007, while he was enrolled in a Composition I course I taught at NSCC. While living in Neptune Towers, he maintained his tribal and familial connections to his Nigerian homeland and found his community therein. He told me that in his home, he teaches his children the Igbo language, he cooks fufu, and on Christmas and Easter, he takes his family to a Nigerian church.

Miguel Soto

MIGUEL SOTO'S ALLEY ST.

My family came over from the Dominican Republic in the 70s. I was born in '76. I was about three years old when my mother came to Boston because we had family members here, and that visit turned into staying in Lynn.

My daughter came along on January 26, 1996, she's three years old now, and after living on Western Ave., my daughter, her mother and myself moved to 162 Alley St., and we lived there for a year and a half. Everybody kept to themselves on that street; nobody really was in anybody else's business. Just the lady downstairs; she was in everybody's business.

The only people that you see down there is the people who kept up their houses, which was from behind Lynn Tech to down where I was, which was by East Coast Seafood. That's the people who kept up with their yard work, snow removal, because from there on, you'll notice they're all renting, none of 'em really owned their apartments.

Further down, what there was was a lot of auto body shops and, um, my friend owns one of them. He owns Diamond Auto Body and I work down there. And I also have a friend that lived next door, oh—not lived, I'm sorry, who had a shop next door; it was a mechanic's shop. Marcellino's—that's the name of the mechanic. I still go there. He's a good mechanic.

Most of the people on Alley St. were old, not in the sense of ancient old, old in the sense of maybe 55, 60 years old, old in my point of view, 'cause I'm young. I'm only 22. So, usually you didn't see too much of their faces; it was just you see them leave in the morning, come back, and that's all. You see them walk their dog, just go out for a walk and then come right back. It's not the type of community that everybody knocks on each other's door: "Hey! What's up? Can I borrow a pan?" Blah, blah, blah. Nothin' like that.

It was a tight community—just that one little block. Everybody kept to themselves, but you see them keeping up their yard work and all that like I said before.

WHEN TO CALL THE COPS

Some other parts of Lynn, somebody could have a fight, they could have a full out brawl before the cops come. But here, if someone is even arguing, they call the cops because they don't want that sort of stuff in their neighborhood. 'Cause of their kids; they know their kids are there, and they just want to get it over with. Somebody's arguing—have the cops come—get 'em outta there—everything's back to normal in half an hour.

Other parts of Lynn, the neighbors just come outside, watch the fight, let everything happen, let 'em all fight and then go ahead—call the cops. When they want people to go home, when the fight's over, they call the cops.

Alley St. was tight in bein' they don't want no problems in their community. If there's a problem in your house, I'll call the cops. And that's all there is to it.

Tight in the way that "I'll call the cops for you, and if it happens with me, call the cops for me." Tight.

THE IRONIC THING

The heat was electric. Baseboards. In the summer the bills came to $180. *In* the summer, the electric bill. In the summer. In the winter, I got one bill, came to $450. One bill, one month. We did that for a while. I had a good-paying job but it wasn't good enough to pay $450 each month, so I had to move from there. I got backtracked one month and the landlord was all over me. He was like, "Arrgh, you're gonna hafta leave."

I say: "I been here for a year paying you $975 a month and now, 'cause I miss one month, you're gonna give me all this trouble?" "I got bills to pay." You know, this and that. So he was just really comin' around every day, so you know what, finally I just said, "I quit," and I moved out of there. He was just harassing. Toward the end of it, the ironic thing is that the guy, the owner, lost his house 'cause he owed back taxes.

KEEPING UP CARS ON ALLEY STREET

Marcellino's the auto mechanic, he did one of my cars there. Then I had bought an '88 RX7 with a rotary engine, and this car was giving me so many problems. He was next door. So one day I wind up having to push my car from my house to the mechanic next door so he can get it fixed. And he had a thing where he said, "Listen—this and this is wrong with it." He didn't try to overcharge me. I said, "I'm in financial difficulty." "No problem." He helped me out. He's a straightforward guy; he'll tell you how much it costs. He don't, after he does it, go: "Oh gee, I put this in there… and that." He don't do the job until you tell him, "OK, go ahead and do it."

I had my car painted over at Diamond. I met him through a friend who had his car painted and it came out all right so I said, "Sure, I'll take my car there." I had a '94 Mazda 626, and I got a good paint job on it, the guy did a real good job. And after that, I bought a Honda Accord from the shop and that car was a lemon. Everything started going on it and he said, "OK. You did buy the car from me; I'll fix it for free," and we just started to be friends. I've taken a lot of people there and he's given them good prices. Sometimes I'll go there like if I need advice with what's wrong with the car. He'll tell me and then say, "I'll do it for free."

LYNN IS A DOMINICAN TOWN

Same as New York City,
there's a lot of Dominicans in town.
You always see them with the little Dominican flags
hanging from the rear-view mirror.
I got one of those—
always.
I'm always calling my family in the Dominican Republic,
sending money every time I can.

RICE AND BEANS

I was raised on it
I will never go from it
I eat to this day
rice and beans
every day of the week

it could be a holiday
rice and beans

if it ain't rice and beans on the plate
I don't have a meal

rice goes with everything
rice and eggs
rice and ketchup
it's rice with everything

they put rice in soup
they make this one soup
it has so much rice in it
they make rice pudding
there's so many things they do with rice

it's unbelievable
even through your ears
rice rice rice
everywhere I go
I have to have my rice and beans

Gary Abdul

COMING TO LYNN

My father came here thirty years ago
when he was just a kid.
They lived somewhere on Elm St.
and eventually they moved to Vine St.,
where my father bought the house.
I wasn't up here at the time.
I lived in Jamaica for the first nine years of my life
and then they just decided that they wanted me up here
to get a better education to further myself in life.

I came up here on the airplane,
Continental Airlines I think it was, and…
it was somewhat of a shock
because when I left it was so warm and when I got here
it was like the middle of win—
I think it was the coldest day that year.

I came out of the plane, going outside,
snow all over the place, ice,
and I'd never seen snow before.
I'd only seen it on tv and the first time
I asked my aunt, "What was that white stuff
falling from the sky on tv?"
She told me, "It's snow."
I'm like, "Well, what is it?"

URBAN RENEWAL 2.0

My dad is a software engineer for Digital Equipment Corporation.
My father likes the neighborhood, but every now and then,
due to the changing of people in certain apartment buildings on our street,
he will complain.
People will stay for like two years or a year and at the end of Vine St.,
there are two gray apartment buildings opposite each other
and the people there have been there a long time,

the longest of any apartment building.

He talks about when there used to be a bar on the corner
and people would fight all the time and you could never go to sleep.
Stuff like that; every now and then he'll come up with a tidbit.

In the summertime, there'd be some old guys out on the street,
under a tree, drinking, yelling, blah, blah, blah.
They'd carry on and you'd hear them miles away.
But we don't really have that problem anymore because
where they used to sit under the tree was an empty lot
and they put a nice house there.

And most of the other empty lots that were there have houses.
Those new houses that are going up all over in Lynn:
yellow houses, pink houses, single-family houses.
I don't know if you've seen them,
but they're all over the place.

INVISIBILITY

It's like if I go into a store,
and I think it has to do with not only race prejudice,
but age prejudice too.

'Cause I've gone with a bunch of my friends
to buy something and people ignore you.
If you ask for help, they ignore you.

You go in to buy something
for a friend or a family member
and they pick another person first.
They go around,
show them whatever they want
and then they take someone else
and then they go on
until there's no one left
before they bring you
to see what you want.

LATE ONE NIGHT ON VINE ST.

Most people on Vine St.
haven't lived here too long
but the people that have,
like my neighbor
and the neighbor across the street,
we help each other out.

Like this summer,
my cousins were over visiting
and we kept hearing a screech all night long
and we finally heard this big screech and a crash.
I thought it was a car hitting another car
since it sounded like sheet metal crumbling.
So I went to my living room window
and the house was on fire.
A car had hit the house.
The engine was on fire
and it was melting our siding.

So I got everyone out: upstairs
my little cousin who was up with me
all night because he wanted to wrestle
and downstairs: my grandmother and my two girl cousins.

So we're all outside and this car is smashed
onto the outside of our house.
And people are yelling at us:
"He's over there! He's over there! He's over there!"
trying to tell us where the driver was
and some people actually went after him.

But he was too fast.
I guess he was running out of fear
'cause we later found out the car was stolen
and it looked like the guy was drunk.
His car was so smashed up
I don't know how he survived.

There was also a passenger that ran away
and people were chasing him too.
I found it funny that people were out that late.
Everyone was out real quick, telling us what happened,
helping the cops get a handle on things.

I must have called the cops ten times,
I was so nervous.
And I asked for an ambulance 'cause
I was concerned for the guy's safety
and he just ran away.

And this car—the hood was missing.
The roof of the car wound up on my uncle's lawn.
The car went under his porch and the roof came off.
Then the car smashed into our house so hard
that when they towed it out,
the license plate stayed stuck onto our house wall.

This was 1:00, 1:30 A.M.
I was totally mad.
The guy hit our house and my uncle's house.
On my uncle's house he hit the porch stairs
and I built those stairs with my uncle.
I built those stairs and they weren't even
attached to the porch anymore.
They were knocked out and they flew
and they landed on my lawn.
They were all knocked to pieces,
but they landed like perfectly on our lawn,
just almost stacked.

Brandy Soto

Doing a Machine's Job

I had a main job
a full-time job in a clothing store in Somerville
and I left it to go back to school
so I needed a job with a better schedule
so through a friend of mine I heard about the job at Lynn Plastics.
He told me it was a good job
that the seven-to-seven shift was easy.
So you know I thought, "Why not.
Let me give it a try." So I go and I fill out a' application
and I got hired right away.
They told me to start the same day;
I told them I'd rather start tomorrow.
So whatever,
they started me the next day.

And honestly
it was the worst job I ever had.
I was like a machine
just going from one position to the next position
no type of using my mind
just like a machine   you know what I'm saying
putting these plastics into a box
just moving these plastics from side to side
you know what I'm saying   just moving my hand.

And the thing that bothered me the most
you know I just wanted to work
the thing that bothered me the most there
they pay you four twenty-five
you know for four twenty-five a job's a job
but for four twenty-five they had me there like a machine
you know what I'm saying   just doing a machine's job.

I was standing in the same place
and I would have to pick up these plastics and put 'em in a box
pick up the plastics   put 'em in a box
pick up the plastics   and then I had to close the box
and then put the boxes in a stack like fifty.

And then after that one of the managers would come and take the stack
and then you would have to start doing another,
but the thing is if you didn't move the plastics right away into the box
the machine would clog up   you know what I'm saying
by my second day the machine was clogging up constantly.

There's a bunch of weird people working in there
you know what I'm saying
one dude was eating constantly
he was skinny   bony
every minute he had something in his mouth
really skinny   I couldn't understand it
everybody's like immigrants
they don't have no papers
the whole environment was just no good
the place was all dirty.

It smelled   it was hot
and then I had to take these boxes
and just be movin' them like an animal.
You didn't have no type of input;
you might as well have been a machine
just programmed to do the job.
Well, whatever.
I did it for a week and then I saw my check.
I got paid a little over a hundred dollars for well over forty hours
and that was my job.
I was embarrassed.
You know I work, but not for four twenty-five
doing that type of job.
You know maybe in McDonald's for four twenty-five, alright,
but yo, this was hard work.
This was hard work so I really wasn't with it too much.

Then you know I eventually got fired.
The next week I went to work and I got
in at seven and they gave me my break
at 7:15 in the morning.
At the end of the day, it was like 6:30,
a half hour before the shift change,
and you can't leave until the next guy gets there
and the guy that's relieving me, he was always late,
and shoot, it was getting me mad,
so around 6:30 I was listening to my headphones
I had my coat on   I had my bookbag on
I was ready to go and I was writing rhymes

and my boss came over and he was like,
"You know, you gotta take off your coat,"
and I was like, "Whiiyyy! You know, chill man.
Don't give me no stress. I'm just here to do my job.
Let me do my job and I'll be out."

I wasn't getting paid enough for him to stress me
so when I was on my way out the door, he was like,
"You know Brandy, I don't think this job's for you."
I was like, "Yo, no kidding, but it's all good.
I'll see you tomorrow. I just want my check. It's all good.
I think you're right. It's not for me."

And that was my episode at the plastics
and I never went back after that.
You know, I wouldn't suggest it to nobody at all,
not even to my enemy to work there.

Russ Tansey

Neptune Towers

Basically, when they tore down the old neighborhood to make room for the new trade school, they built Neptune Towers, which, I don't know, call it a Lynn skyscraper. Basically, everyone in the Brickyard who was disposed ended up in Neptune Towers. And it lost that neighborhood community feeling. And the classic case is my cousin passed away; he was dead in his apartment for two weeks before anyone found him. That wouldn't have happened in the old neighborhood. Someone would have asked, "Where's Ralph?"

My grandmother, and pretty much everyone who lived on Dowling Terrace ended up in Neptune Towers. My grandmother, my great aunt, my cousin, my other great aunt. It was a very sterile environment. Any time you live in a high-rise complex it's, there's no sense of community in a situation like that. Having gone from a close tight-knit community to a high-rise building—it changes the dynamics of the relationships of people. You only see them if perchance you get on the same elevator. And that's about the only time you're gonna see them. Back then, there was no air conditioning, so hot summers, you sat out on the porch or the stoop.

Leah Levitin

ENGLISH

1

I didn't try to know any people because of my English first
I could not speak   I can   maybe speak this year
This summer a little bit   start to, this is first course
I just could not speak

When I first came, it was terrible thing
Can I use my dictionary?
Mmm, mute, it looks like mute
Yah exactly   I could not speak any simple word
Simple asks about what time
or about I need to buy something
I couldn't speak anything   even a little
I like those place where I don't need to speak English
For example, Star Market
not a lot of person to talk to

I watched television a lot   I read a lot
books for begin   It helped me
but it was inside me   potential
I couldn't speak orally
but I knew a lot of words   English words
but I could not use them

Sometime my friend have little knewing words
but they speak more freely
with small English vocabulary
My daughter speaks English with me most most
but very often I need to ask her
"Say it again. Say it again. I don't understand."
Sometimes I understand that good but sometimes not

Jewish Community Center, ah, ah,
Chairperson   now she is retired
she came in my house
just to see how I live
begin to live here, and say hello
and she help to send me to temple
for learning my English
That was my first school
English, it took one year   at Temple Beth-El
One year
Then I took three months in Lynn close to Neptune
It was different there
It's not Jewish exactly, because of different people
Chinese people and different people
Bennett St. Bennett St.   yah

And after this three months
my friend said we need to try study in college
take profession
This is just my Russian friend
I met her here in neighborhood
She lives in Neptune too, in the Towers
Ah, I remember   First I met her in Temple Beth-El
She came there for English too
but her English was more better
and I saw her maybe two times   But we met after that
and we a lot of talk about what we need to do

And my good friend tells me
"You need to go. You must go."
and really helped me
And I had really hard time in studying
and sometime I thought I need to give up
I thought maybe I fail out, it's so easy for me to give up
but it doesn't happen
But now I close on nursing
Now I feel I can handle it and I don't
I don't want to give up it
and I will try continue and I hope maybe I did it
I will do it

Alex Kaplan

THE KAPLANS COME TO NEPTUNE TOWERS

1

My aunt came here from Ukraine in '92 and she invited us and we had to go through the procedure, like two or three years. We had to make all the papers and that was a big process.

We flew from Kyiv to Helsinki, from Helsinki to New York, and from New York we came to Boston. And then we came to an apartment my aunt had rented out for us on West Baltimore St.

Then we applied to live in Neptune Towers and we were lucky. We waited only eight months. And when we came in, a guy who was in the elevator asked how long it took us to get in and we said, "Eight months," and he goes, "Did you bribe somebody?" He had to wait three and a half years.

We came December 5, 1994, six years ago yesterday. My aunt lived in Neptune Towers on the twelfth floor East. She waited a year and half, something like that.

2

My grandfather woke me up one night at five o'clock in the morning. My mother was screaming, yelling, "Don't ask me questions." We had probably sixteen bags, huge bags.

In New York nobody came to help us; we were like late for the plane, but it was a special Russian community thing. We had to watch something, get our papers, and me, my grandfather and my brother, we were trying to move those sixteen bags from one terminal to another. There were eight of us.

And when we drove from the airport to West Baltimore and we were on the Lynnway, there were so many cars. "Who buys all these cars?" I thought. In Russia you stand in line to buy a car, but here there were parking lots full of cars. Cars everywhere.

And then we came to our building. It was old. That was my first impression. And then there was a building to the side of it that had burned down. It was all black and the side of our building was white-gray.

We live on the sixth floor West. Our apartment is three bedrooms; my brother and I have our own bedroom, which we didn't have in Kyiv. On West Baltimore St., my parents were in the bedroom and we were in the guest room.

My grandfather lives on the eighth floor on my side and my grandmother, not my grandfather's wife, lives here too in her own apartment.

Dima Kuperman

ANTISEMITISM IN UKRAINE: THE LAST STRAW

It was very hard to live in Odessa, not actually Odessa, but Ukraine itself. Odessa had a big Jewish population, but in Ukraine, Jews were not liked. A lot of times they were hated, and if you were Jewish, you wouldn't get a good education. You had to bribe people; you would be persecuted. So that's why we decided to come to the U.S.

For example, I went to this school. It wasn't a big problem with most of the people, but one person exceptionally hated Jews. He just happened to be very strong you know; I couldn't kick his butt. I had to kind of deal with it. He would call me names all the time. And why we moved is because if I stayed there and I'm Jewish, I couldn't get into a university, even if I knew a lot more than a Russian or Ukrainian person.

They even told my father when he was trying to get in for journalism, "We're not making journalists for Israel." He was like, "What? I'm not moving to Israel. I'm staying here." "We don't care." That's what they told him. Here in the U.S., it would be impossible to say that.

We finally moved because one of my neighbors, back in the Ukraine, he went into the Russian army, the Ukrainian army, and they made him an invalid. They almost killed him just because he was Jewish. He came back and would have operations like twice a month to try to fix him. My parents saw that and they were like, "We're not staying here."

ALL DIFFERENT

As soon as I walked out of the airline terminal, everything seemed different because it was. People looked different, everybody dressed different and everything was more high-tech. Everything was more advanced. It was like stepping into a movie. In the Ukraine, I would watch movies of the U.S., and now I'm here. All the buildings are different; the cars are all different.

In all the American movies, there would be a huge supermarket people would go in. It looked really cool, you know, and in Russia it would be a little store and you wouldn't actually go in. You would say, "I want that." You would point and they would bring it to you. It would waste a lot of time.

Here the first time I went to a big supermarket, it was Star Market, close to Neptune Boulevard. I was like, "Wow! This is the biggest place I've ever seen." It was a completely different kind of market. In the Ukraine, there were no supermarkets; people were afraid stuff was gonna get stolen. In America, the problem of shoplifting isn't that big and people trust each other more. It was amazing to see stuff being laid out all over the place and no one trying to steal.

OUR WAY TO NEPTUNE TOWERS

Our decision to come to Lynn wasn't actually a decision. The fact was our relatives were living in Lynn, and we came to the U.S. under the condition that we would be reunited with our relatives and at the same time escape persecution. So we came to Lynn because it would be a lot cheaper to get an apartment here and it's cheaper to live.

So we came to Lynn on October 18, 1994, and the first thing we did was to stay over with relatives until we decided which apartment we wanted to rent. We rented an apartment on Green St. in the white Harvard-Yale building. And because of the high rent there, we decided to rent an apartment in Neptune Towers.

The apartments were big and they were subsidized. For example, you only pay 30% of your income. It didn't matter how much you made; you only paid 30%.

The size of the apartment would depend on the size of your family, so it wouldn't matter if you got a one-bedroom apartment, a studio or a three-bedroom apartment. You still paid 30%, so that was very nice.

We would pay less for a two-bedroom apartment than our one-bedroom and I would get my own room for the first time in my life. So we put in an application for Neptune Towers and it took about a year and a half for us to get in.

MY OWN ROOM

It feels really nice to have my own room. Your room is like your piece of the world.

When we moved in, all the furniture, it was stuff that people gave us. We didn't buy much stuff because we didn't have a lot of money. So it was just a bunch of junk all over the place. But my parents did buy me a computer so I could learn a profession. And that helped out a lot—I'm going into computer engineering. Then I got a cheap stereo system—it wasn't cheap, it was eighty bucks—but it's not good.

The last few months or so, I threw all of that out. Now I'm working and buying good stuff. I got a new computer; I bought all the new furniture. I bought a 57" tv, which is like too big for that room; it's like a meter and a half. I got a 400-watt stereo system with five speakers, VCR, everything. I just wanted to get the best.

When I moved in, I thought the more random stuff all over the place the better. I put little pictures of cars all over the place. It was unbelievable. Every piece of the wall there was something.

But now I think it doesn't look that good. So I'm going more into stylish stuff. Now I tore all that stuff down and I'm only putting up stuff in frames. I went to the store and I got a picture of a Diablo; it's a red car, beautiful, it's beautiful and it's in a gold frame. It looks nice, very presentable. I'm doing that stuff now, and I'm making it look more contemporary you know, more grown up.

LIVING IN NEPTUNE TOWERS

1

Basically, I didn't know anyone when I moved in. The first person I became acquainted with was also Russian and his grandfather was my barber in Odessa. He's the same age as I am and we became very good friends and I'm still friends with him

Before, a friend of mine lived here—Igor—he lived right across from me—he moved to Salem Willows. He's older than I am. I definitely talk to him when I meet him, but I don't hang out with him. He's an acquaintance.

Alex Kaplan lives on the sixth floor in my building and his father and my father are very good friends. And I'm friends with his brother Dima. Again he's older than me. I talk to him; he's an acquaintance. We talk about cars.

2

A lot of the kids my age—17, 16 and 15—they have their grandparents living in the Towers, so for example, if they lived in Swampscott, they would sometimes stay over with their grandparents on the weekends so we can hang out. But now it's not really needed. We all have cars now. We can just drive back and forth so it really doesn't matter. Neptune Towers is not a hang-out spot. I just live there.

The neighborhood of Neptune Towers brought some benefits to me though. For example, I like the parking lot of Neptune Towers because I like to see my car out of my window. I like the fact there is a field there that I can use to run around, play soccer. That's a nice field. And then my driving lessons started in the parking lot opposite Neptune Towers at Lynn Tech. And there's another parking lot and in that one I learned how to drive standard. That was pretty cool.

3

I don't talk to many people who live in Neptune Towers, even Russian people. I just talk to my friends. I don't really sit around Neptune Towers. I don't use it as my hang-out spot. For the main reason that I can't.

For example, if I wanted my friends to come over, there is no room that we could sit down in. Some apartments and condos when you come in, there is a little room with sofas and a tv that you can sit down in and talk with each other. There is nothing like that here, so it's really made to just go into your apartment and live there.

4

Getting along is definitely not a problem. I have neighbors who are Black; I talk to them sometimes you know. I'm not friends with any of my neighbors. It's fine. We get along. It's never any problem. There is some stuff that goes on.

Like once, well I think it was two months ago, some woman jumped out of her balcony in the other building on the ninth floor and there was all cops there. They circled everything off. They wouldn't let anybody out. They needed to talk to everyone. And then there was like a shooting five years ago. Someone killed someone. Just stuff. It goes on. You can't get around that.

I've never seen someone go out into the hall and someone else would go out and they would talk to each other. There is no space to do that. The halls look very cold. It looks like a prison you know. You walk in. The halls are like long and narrow. If the doors are swung out into the hallway, they would probably hit each other. It doesn't seem warm and inviting; it seems more cold and prisonly.

5

There is no neighborly organization. There is a function room, which you have to rent out. You have to pay a $35 deposit, which is fine, but you have to be out of there by 9:00. It's stupid. For example, if I like to hold my birthday party there, and I want to say have like loud music and party with my friends, I have to be kicked out by 9:00, which is stupid. It's the time everybody would come.

People just talk to their friends. There are no organizations. There are no tenant organizations I know of. Everything is controlled by the rental people. They control everything. The owners, the subsidy people, they control everything.

THE PEOPLE TRY TO CONTROL YOU

The maintenance people live in the building.
They get free rent or something.
They're real annoying.

The maintenance people—I can't stand them.
They get into stuff that isn't their business.
I was doing modifications to my car.
I got some stuff
and I wasn't ruining the parking lot or anything,
I just opened my hood.
I was installing an air intake,
and a maintenance person comes up to me
and they're like, "What are you doing?"
I'm like, "What? I'm not spilling oil
in the parking lot so what's the problem?"
They're like, "Oh, you're not supposed to do
any modifications."
I'm like, "All right. Whatever,"
and I just drove off to the Lynn Tech parking lot
and did it there.

The bad part of Neptune Towers is that
the people try to control you.
For the low rent that they give you,
they do monthly inspections
of the building, of your apartment.
They check out if you're a nice housekeeper.
For example, they don't want the walls
to be like torn down.
They don't want you to touch anything.
For example, you would get a huge fine
if you let's say put a nail in the door
to hang a coat or something.

Sometimes when I hang out, like around 1:00 A.M.,
when we drive down to the parking lot
like with my friends with a couple of cars,
you know security comes up to us
and they're like, "What are you doing here?"
And I'm like, "I live here."
And he's like, "Well, why are you here so late?"
I'm like, "What?" and they ask to see my parking permit
like they think they're in charge.

EVERYTHING IS TOGETHER PRETTY WELL

The buildings seemed alright
from the outside but inside
it was all weird.

They constantly paint the halls.
I have no idea why that is.
Is there lead paint they need to cover up?
I have no idea what's going on.
That doesn't bother me.

Generally, it looks well maintained.
Every time someone moves out of an apartment,
the maintenance crew comes in
and they repaint the walls.
They clean everything out.
They repaint the front door you know.
I've never seen graffiti on Neptune Towers.
Every time something goes wrong,
there is a maintenance crew who lives there
and they'll take care of it you know.

Everything is well maintained.
The grass is always trimmed.
A crew comes in—
some landscape company—
black trucks
I'm not sure what the name is
with green lettering.
They come and they trim the grass;
they mow the lawn.
They take care of that
and they spray the grass with pesticides.

Neptune Towers and Other Russian Places

1

A lot of Russians live here. A lot of people jokingly call it Russian projects. There's a lot of older Russian population because the younger population buys homes after a while, which I plan to do also.

Every family is connected to Neptune Towers because let's say their grandparents lived there, or they lived there at some point in their life, so everyone knows Neptune Towers. Anyone in the Russian community, if you say, "I live in Neptune Towers," they say, "Oh, I know exactly where that is." It's a kind of a Russian place.

2

The older population likes it here because they don't have to pay as much rent and also it's nice protection for them since let's say if two elderly people live together and one of them dies, then their rent is gonna go down, and they can easily, well not easily, they can support themselves instead of having to go to a retirement home or something like that and find a way to pay for it. Here the rent would go down and they could pay for it, so it's a pretty nice place.

The older Russian people hang out together. On that parking lot there are a couple of benches, a couple more, like ten. They're lined up along the buildings, they're a bunch of them right here, and people talk to each other. They sit there you know, and some of the older Russian population have cars, like some of the men you know, in Russia they didn't drive a lot, some of the men have cars, and when someone needs to go somewhere, they drive them. Everybody tries to help each other.

Most of the people sitting are Russian. Sometimes you see others, but most of the time it's Russian people. Out of both of the buildings, it would seem that 50% of the people living there are Russian. The other 50% are a low-income population that have lived here for a long time—a lot of Spanish people there, Black people there. They're my neighbors.

3

In Lynn, there are two Russian stores. One is near Neptune Towers; it's near Star Market. It's called Foods of Europe. It's run by my relative, and then there is another Russian store on Broad St. I have no idea what that one's called; they call it by the name of the owner, so that's Lenny's store on Broad St. Then there are Russian hairdressers; there are two of them. There is a Russian pharmacy; there are two. One is near Foods of Europe; one is near Lenny's.

There is a Russian restaurant. It's near the Lynnway. I go there all the time. It's a very expensive restaurant and it's called Mirage. It looks horrible from the outside, but once you walk in, it's unbelievable. They don't spend much money on the outside. I mean people come there at 10:00 P.M. and no one looks at the outside. I don't know, it looks like a warehouse. Then you walk in—everything is done beautifully. So it's a nice place.

4

Then there's a Russian hangout in Dunkin' Donuts on the Lynnway. A lot of Russian friends hang out there because in the winter it's cold, so we walk in, we buy donuts, whatever. And in the summer we hang out in the parking lot near Nahant, the Causeway near the rotary. We hang out there because a lot of Russian people like cars. We have our cars there; we look at them. Then there is a Russian hangout we got to know; it's in Newton. I'm trying to get out of the neighborhood.

I'M PROUD OF MY RELIGION

By the time I was leaving Odessa, there was only one synagogue and it wasn't getting enough funding and it was almost closed down. We didn't light candles on Hanukkah because first of all, you couldn't buy them there. They sold matzo, but they didn't sell anything else. That made it almost impossible to observe your religion and the other reason that made it impossible: Let's say if I wore a Jewish star, like I do most of the time here, there—I would probably get shot. People would make fun of me all the time.

Here in Lynn it's a lot better. I'm proud of my religion. I went to Israel about one and a half years ago in the summer of '99. I explored my religion; I was there for a month with a program.

But I'm not observant. I mean you have to, if you want to observe your religion, you have to do it from the time you are born. That has to be in your family. But it wasn't in my family so I was kind of alien to all that they were doing in Israel and sometimes it would seem boring to me because I wasn't used to it. I don't even know the language.

SECURITY

Both towers of Neptune Towers are identical,
but at the other tower,
not mine, 130 East,
there is a security station,
which is responsible for the parking lot,
for the cars there and the stuff that goes on
in the buildings. I don't think they
are that good because there are cars
stolen from the parking lot all the time.

My bedroom window looks out to the parking lot.
The reason I park my car right near my window,
like I said there was a car a little further over
and you couldn't see it out of the window—
it was stolen—the security there—everything—
it was stolen.

So I have my car here near my window
for security reasons.
If someone tries to steal it,
I'm going to hear the alarm.

Kenechukwu (Kenneth) Ofonagoro

KEN OFONAGORO'S BRICKYARD

1

I have a friend in the West Tower.
He is the person who introduced me to the Neptune Tower.
He is from Ghana, but he has lived in Nigeria before.
He too drives cars; that is our profession.

Sometimes we meet and we'll be talking about life over here
and I was telling him how I want to get a cheaper apartment
so it won't be very difficult when my family comes.
So he said it's better that I come and register there
and if it's time and I'm lucky, I might get it.

2

Neptune Tower is far better than Summer St.
Summer St. had a lot of problem—
parking space… they don't have parking space.
A couple of times they hit my car while I park it on the street.
My friend who was living downstairs was robbed.
It was a very bad neighborhood.
And I come from work every day late,
so when I come home, I'm always scared about
what if somebody will attack me?

Neptune Tower is very nice.
We have parking space.
We have everything.
It's a very good neighborhood.
They have security there.
They have camera everywhere.
You don't see people moving around you know
just passing or something like that.
You can't get in through the lobby without
somebody buzzing you in.

THE ORLU PROGRESSIVE ASSOCIATION

1

When I came here newly I was very lonely,
staying only with my cousin
and my cousin is always going to work you know
so I wasn't you know enjoying it… I like to go out.
Eventually I met somebody, I've forgotten his name,
so you know he told me they have association here
and he would like me to come.
At that time there were very few,
there were just like fifteen or something like that.
We have like in Nigeria
we have the community here
our senatorial zone community
which is OPA, our local association.
The association—everybody there is Igbo
because it's a tribal association.

2

Actually I'm the secretary of my people
and I try to make sure our association is a very strong one.
We are now about 47 members.
Every month one person will host us
and to celebrate the meeting,
we make sure the person will prepare our local food for us.
At least fifty percent has to be our local food.

3

And we discuss about how we are going
to make our association here strong
and the way to help people back home.
'Cause we do monthly contributions
and sometimes we have some money
and anybody that is going home
we give him some money and make sure he go home
and he do something in his home locality.
Like last year I think we sponsored about four people
and we give them like one thousand,

one thousand five hundred dollars,
so that when they go home,
they use it to do some project
and when they do that
they have to let the people know
that it is we here that sponsor the project.

4

Some people when they go home they will,
because over there they have a lot of problems like water,
they don't have steady water supply,
so sometimes they will use that money to dig more hole
and make sure that, you know, water comes out from there.
Sometimes if the money is not enough,
some of them can put a lot of money from their own person
to get water to provide water for their people.

5

Some people can use it because,
maybe the electricity is not standard to their area,
use it to buy some electricity poles and the wires to make sure electricity
you know, you know, reached to their area.

Sometimes some people use it, like primary schools in the area,
they use it to sponsor one thing or the other,
like soccer and good educational facilities for them.
They mending the walls, the old ones.
They have such projects you know.

MY FATHER. MY HOMELAND.

1

I like any music that, you know,
the rhythm is good to me.
My father is a talented musician
although he never played to make money.
He plays everything about music. Guitar—
anything at all he handles; he plays it very well.
In our village he's known for that,
so that is where my kids are getting their talent.

2

I try to go home once every year.
Last year I went home because my father died.
I am the first son.
He has other people, like my senior sister,
but I am the first boy.
Traditionally, when such a thing happens,
the first sons are supposed to be around.
People use it to value people, to see that you are doing well,
to know your value.

If you cannot, if you are the first son
and you are not around to bury your father,
people, you know, put some special mark on it.
You are not doing well or you are stuck somewhere.
You have to go and bury your father.
I tried. I went to him last year to bury him.

This year, next month, we are going to do the memorial
because he was buried on 8th of June last year.
We are going to do the memorial service
and that will require me again to be around.
So hopefully I am trying to make sure that
I will be able to do that memorial service and come back.

THE BRICKYARD BRAND: 21ˢᵀ CENTURY CREATIVE ENTREPRENEURS

The Gold

The suddenness flowers have
startles the air
with their fire and ether
as we do with what is ours
because we are
the gardeners of each other

—Vincent Ferrini
I Have the World [1967]

1

In 2004, Kathryn Grover answered the question, "What happened to the Brickyard?" in the title of her book, *The Brickyard: The Life, Death, and Legend of an Urban Neighborhood*. In Grover's view, the post-urban renewal Brickyard was a ghost of its former self, kept alive by the memories of pre-urban renewal residents. In 2020, my answer to the question, "What happened to the Brickyard?" is that it still exists as a shrunken neighborhood and an expanding brand.

2

Geographically, physically, the Brickyard can be found today in the residential parts of the area between the Lynnway and the Commuter Rail tracks, and, depending on your opinion, maybe also north of Summer St. between Shepard St. and Commercial St. Undeniably, the heart of today's Brickyard is along Harbor St. and Alley St., where the traditions of the Brickyard before urban renewal survive at the Italian American Citizens Club on Harbor St. and at DiFillipo's Brickyard Bar & Grill on Blossom St. Read the essay "Brickyard 2020" for more about today's Brickyard.

North of Summer St, one block up on Shepard St., is June Lane, the cul-de-sac containing Brickyard Village. Described in greater depth in the essay "From Urban Renewal to Neighborhood Development," Brickyard Village, built in 2005, is a great example of the creative capacity of Lynn Housing Authority and Neighborhood Development to develop affordable housing. But calling these 15 garden apartment units Brickyard Village doesn't quite create a new Brickyard as much as show how the name has become a brand. Additional uses of the Brickyard name as a brand in the years following urban renewal include Brickyard VFX, the hip-hop trio The Brickyard, the Brickyard Collaborative maker space and the performer calling himself The Brickyard Prince.

3

Today, the spirit of the Brickyard animates the endeavors of some 21st century creative entrepreneurs who adopt the Brickyard as a brand and use it as a source of inspiration. In 2019, I interviewed six men, each a creative entrepreneur in his own way, each using the Brickyard brand to imbue his work with the essence and vitality of the Brickyard in its heyday. The six speakers are:

Rocco Capano (1969–   )

Rocco embodies both the old Brickyard and the new. He and his family are long-time Alley St. residents. His brother Peter represents the Brickyard area in the Massachusetts legislature and his father is considered the epitome of the old Brickyard by Fred Hogan and Jason Taglieri, who also tell their stories in this section. I interviewed Rocco in his recording studio on March 20, 2019, and I really enjoyed being with Rocco in that setting.

Rocco personifies the tradition of creativity among Brickyarders. He is a multi-talented sound artist, oil painter, documentary filmmaker, hip-hop musician and producer whose work is influenced by a lifetime spent in the Brickyard.

Rocco's collaboration with two other Lynn hip-hop musicians was called The Brickyard, and his CD, "10 Red Rocks," which exemplifies Rocco's use of collage in service of his hip-hop sound artistry, was copyrighted by Brickyard Beats. "The Roc's in Your Head, part 1," available on vimeo.com, expounds Rocco's views on the art of hip-hop, while part 2 includes images of the Brickyard sign on Blossom St. as well as aerial footage of the neighborhood. More of Rocco's self-produced music videos are on YouTube.

The importance to Rocco of neighborhood preservation is shown in his short documentaries, "Nahant is Not For Sale" and "The Last Little Italy," both of which can be seen on vimeo.com. Also on vimeo.com are the short documentaries "Honor the Saints" and "Feast of All Feasts," which, like "The Last Little Italy," are driven by Rocco's affinity for Boston's North End. They also show Rocco's reverence for saints, something reflected in his love and respect for the memory of his grandfather.

Jason Taglieri (1974–   )

On April 13, 2019, I interviewed Jason at a space being developed for Centerboard, a social service agency whose mission is to "empower families, young people and communities for success." He was excited about what the new facility, located in City Hall Square, would do for Lynn. Jason is a musician and was a member of The Brickyard. Like Rocco Capano, Jason wants to work collaboratively and nurture the artistic work of others.

Fred Hogan (1970–   )

I met Fred at the Lynn Museum and that led to my interview with him at Lynn's Land of a Thousand Hills Coffee Co. on March 19, 2019. A former DJ, he suggested I contact Rocco and Jason for additional perspectives on the music scene in the Brickyard and in Lynn. Fred is currently the city councilor who represents the Brickyard area. On his daily runs through the neighborhood, he connects with his constituents. Scrolling through his Facebook postings reveals his involvement with many community events and organizations.

Fred is particularly passionate about and committed to Stop The Violence Lynn and this unfortunately intersected with his love of basketball in the summer of 2019. During the Shoe City Classic tournament, which is held in the Brickyard and which was begun by Fred over 25 years earlier, a shooting occurred, the first instance of violence in the history of the tournament. As reported by *The Boston Globe*, Fred was on the scene right away, tending to one of the injured, and the next day he returned to lead the cleanup of the court on Warren St., after which he said, "Now the kids can come back and use it. We don't want this to be an empty park. We just want people to know that this is your park… your community."

Ted Dillard (1956–   )

On August 11, 2019, I interviewed Ted at the Brickyard Collaborative, the maker space he started in West Lynn. Though not originally from Lynn, Ted views the city as an ideal location for an enterprise that can provide people with tools, opportunity, expertise and a space to create. In the spring and summer of 2020, Ted demonstrated his commitment to his community by mobilizing the assets of the Brickyard Collaborative to produce over four thousand pieces of personal protective equipment to help local health care facilities in their fight against Covid-19.

Dave Waller (1963–   )

I interviewed Dave on April 10, 2019, at the Boston headquarters of Brickyard VFX, the visual effects company he founded in 1999. Dave's grandfather lived in the Brickyard, and for him, just like for Ted, the name Brickyard represents qualities and values he wants his company to embody.

Dave's interest in visual effects goes back to his youthful attraction to neon signs. He has a noteworthy collection and some of them have been publicly exhibited with great fanfare. A collection of twelve of Dave's neon signs entitled "Retrolit" was installed as part of Lynn's first Beyond Walls summer celebration of urban art in 2017. And in May of 2018, a group of eight more of Dave's neon signs was set up for the summer on the Rose Kennedy Greenway in Boston and named "Glow."

Ralph Tufo (1949–   )

I interviewed my long-time colleague at North Shore Community College in his Winthrop, MA home on June 17, 2019. Ralph has played the accordion all his life. He was a member of the Boogaloo Swamis and currently leads the Squeezebox Stompers. Ralph likes to say that as a child he took accordion lessons on State St., just east of Pleasant St., in what became the frozen food aisle of Star Market, a store now vacant.

Ralph grew up on South St. Court, four blocks on the other side of Commercial St. from the Brickyard, but because he attended mass at St. Francis Church and his family members lived in the Brickyard, Ralph has a strong connection to the neighborhood. He remembers trying to buy Theresa the Balloon Lady's star-shaped badge that allowed her to be a street vendor—no deal. Both a playwright and a musician, Ralph has completed his third dramatic musical, "Beyond the Blues," which takes place in a bar in the Brickyard in 1982. There's a lot of the Brickyard in "Beyond the Blues," and the bar could be, but of course isn't, DiFillipo's Brickyard Bar & Grill.

Rocco Capano

My Father

1

He's an overachiever and he came over from Italy. Dragged half the village of San Sostene with him and has always worked two jobs. He was the only son so that gave him determination. Not 'cause he's my father, but I've never seen a more driven person.

He didn't know how to write English; all he knew how to do was add and subtract. My father learned how to speak English while he was working at a job. Other workers, they would write words in the ground and in the dirt and he would remember and collect words: "Oh, that's how you say 'refrigerator.'" "That's how you say…".

2

He likes to build and that's what he got hooked on. He'd get a house and then he'd make it nice and do the yard. If the tenants don't take care of the property, he puts a garden in there. The white house down the street. I remember this. I was a kid. There were people drinking and trash in front of the house. The house next to his house, there was a sign that said, "For Sale." He went up to the house, pulled the sign down and called the guy and bought the house and threw all the people out that were treating… just throwing garbage everywhere and he just fixed that whole section. The whole neighborhood he put trees out front. He goes in the gutter and he gets the weeds out of the cracks.

My father's a creative person. I've grown to know this as I've gotten older. This is just what he knows to do. He sees a house and he makes, he wants to make something of it.

3

He's addicted to shovels. He likes to dig holes. My father once gave me a shovel for Christmas. I said, "What are we gonna do with this?" He said, "Oh, well, plant the tomatoes over here, or there." I wanted Rock 'Em Sock 'Em Robots; he gave me a shovel. But, I know how to plant. I know how to turn soil and all of that.

My Grandfather's Head

1

I've sculpted it, I've painted it in black and white and just every way you can think of 'cause I've always admired him as a man. He never spoke English and my understanding of Italian is very limited. I can't describe it; how can you? We knew how we thought and we were comfortable around each other. We used to hang on the back porch and eat sun-dried tomatoes and he had cheese and he would drink his wine and he just never judged me.

It's a strange life when you're creative because you work like a jackass, and sometimes you have no money and other times when you have money, they don't think you put the time in. It's weird; people that did not understand understand now 'cause I never changed. If you do something long enough, they say, "OK. You're a good guy." They're gonna say okay. My grandfather, he always, he never made me feel like I was, he just loved me for who, what I was, and I can't explain that. He was always happy to see me.

2

When my grandfather died, it's kind of a personal thing, but if you put it down a decent way, it would be nice. This was my grandfather. I'll tell you this. He died in the most special way a human can leave the planet. He had all his grandchildren around him in the bed. His daughter was holding his head. I was looking at this man that I'd painted and sculpted and his last breath of life, he was looking right at me.

He started talking Italian and I guess he was asking his daughter if his sister was on the other side and when she said something in Italian, she was holding him like it was a religious picture, and I guess he knew that and he just boom—died and everybody in that room experienced a loss like you wouldn't, an unexpected explosion of grief and I've never seen my father, that's when I knew what my grandfather meant to my father 'cause he never just showed that type of sadness.

We were in the elevator after, just looking at each other like "Wow—he was loved; he was an unbelievable person." This guy that I painted and drew and memorized. I could sign his face like my name, and you know to have that last breath of life, just looking at that saintly face.

3

To keep the birds out of his grapevine, my grandfather wouldn't like the birds eating the grapes, he used to keep like a stuffed animal, some kind of teddy bear, no it was a lion. Right. It was there for so long, it was part of the whole structure. When he died, I looked in the yard, the grapevine, and I swear the lion's head was looking straight up to the sky. I have a picture of it. The lion is looking straight up.

THE ART OF ART

1

I had an interest in art, but I left that all behind to fun around. Skip school and go to Central Square. A big thing that happened in the 80s was an eccentric guy named Walter Dyer dropped money out of a plane in Central Square and all the kids were on the bridge with nets.

Yeah, you hear the story? It was a big event and he might have done it for publicity; we don't know, but all the kids skipped school and got high and waited for the money to fly down on their heads and it went into the ocean and they were pissed. People were mad at him and he didn't come around for a while after that. Luckily, I got away from just being crazy like that and getting into trouble.

2

The Fourth of July we would have competitions, bonfire competitions throughout the city. It's amazing now to think of it. We used a telephone pole as the centerpiece and we would pull wood off the back of old houses. At one time just about everyone competed: Hood St. by George School, Marian Gardens, East Lynn over by Eastern Junior High School. That was a ritual that lasted until the mid-90s, maybe '93. Lynn would be literally on fire and the fire department was cool with it as long as you didn't throw tires, M80s, or quarter sticks in there. So naturally we would want to throw tires, quarter sticks, and we are lucky we didn't blow each other up.

3

People don't understand it's like a form of spirituality when kids are breaking things, not too maliciously. Like when we were young, we would walk the street and you'd hear the Timberlands dragging off the ground, and I would say, "This is all we're doing in life?" and I would kick a barrel and throw it into a car, not 'cause I cared about hurting the car, I wasn't trying to be malicious, so it was like I wanted them to know other things could happen.

I want something different to happen, something that's not supposed to happen. That's kind of where I'm at now. I'm at a thing where I bring it out of other people and other people bring it out in me and everything is all about that.

See the hip-hop thing, the reason that was so cool was because it wasn't respected in the beginning. It sounded broken. It was like you were not supposed to be doing that. It was a little bit illegal, but then you're making it sound crazy and now it sounds broken and slow and limping along, but then you like the accidental broken nature of it. That's why it's bound to always stay cool.

4

Everything has a collaging nature; my music is a collage. There's something happening: you're going along and then I'll always have something off, or it drops out. Then something at a different time signature will come in or somebody will say something. It's just collage.

I love to look at something that is put together solid and then just shave it down. For instance, I stack drum sounds. Someone will play a drum; I'll whack a board and then I'll put a coffee shaker over it and then I put it in there and then I'll chip the beginning of it so it's not as hard. I like to chip in or out.

I'm always playing. I have my own snares, all my own rims, all my own kicks, all my own and then I have this flinchy thing that I do to the groove where I make it feel old school mentally ill like people that have a twitch. If it has a flinch, then I know the beat is good and it's not perfect and I love it.

Always do something to mess up something perfect which is just a quality that the artists that I love do. They glorify something you would be ashamed of. It's like the craziest thing.

That's what I grew up doing so it's natural to me. To put together a song with other sounds is something that I'll do. Whether there's money involved or not, it's just a natural thing.

COLLABORATION

1

I don't really know what it is, but like the Puerto Ricans are interested in the whites, the whites are interested in the Puerto Ricans, everyone's like, it's more based on what kind of talent you have. White kids are good at spray painting; Puerto Ricans are good at break dancing. So, we are all interested in each other. We don't really think about, "Oh, he is this color. He's that color," 'cause we all grew up together.

2

The Puerto Ricans for instance, they'll try to make something work that shouldn't be and that's the whole essence. I remember one time I was going through my closet, cleaning it out, and this kid Jesse Cruz (we were both DJs), and I had this reverb which I would just never use in my life. It was like a Radio Shack piece of garbage, but he didn't have one and I said, "You want this reverb?" and he looked at me like he had a tear in his eye, he was like, "You would give this to me?" I said, "It's in the closet. I don't care."

When I went to his house, he'd drilled holes in his entertainment stand, put it underneath like he was on the Starship Enterprise, and he ran his whole stereo through the thing. He made all his tapes through this reverb and that gave him his own sound. You knew it was his tape when you heard it because he had the little setting that he liked. Who would do that? But that's the creative impulse and I've always enjoyed that.

3

Musically, there is a friend of mine, kind of like a younger brother. He's very talented, his name is Jay, Jason Taglieri. You might want to talk to him. He's a very humble guy. He used to sit in the studio. He was a younger kid and he wasn't as developed lyrically as some of the other people, but he liked writing and he wanted to make music and he would hang around until everybody left and then he would see if I could show him how to use the equipment and eventually he got his own studio and he has made tons of recorded music.

See, what people don't understand, you spend a lot of time alone and you're in a studio, but you're not alone. It's the most beautiful feeling in the world to call a friend on the phone and say, "Listen to what I did. I got this with that." And then he will show me over the phone something he's doing. So there was this thing between me, Jason, who lives near where the fire station was when I was a kid, Sherwin, who lives up by the Common (he was more into rapping), but mostly Jason and a kid Andre that was from Dorchester. I really enjoy these relationships.

4

I see myself helping people like myself from this area if possible. The ones that you can't get out of the house, they're not going to be at the nonprofit turkey dinner because they're just busy thinking of what else they're gonna do and dodging their family that's going to tell them to get a real job. I love those people.

Jason Taglieri

A Young Man Conscious of Race

My mother is from Revere and my dad is a Lynn native so I'm not sure exactly how we wound up on Shepard St. It was probably just an affordable place to live. After Shepard St., I moved to Oxford Terrace. We were basically right next door to what was the Welfare office at the time. It was a lot of movement coming in and out. A very diverse neighborhood, we had Italian, Greeks, Blacks, Spanish, just the whole gamut living in pretty tight quarters together. So close together that there really weren't like segregated neighborhoods, at least when I was coming up.

My mother is Italian, my father is Black, so it was kind of a unique situation for me growing up 'cause I could see both sides. My mother's family are hardcore Revere Italians and they weren't racist you know, but we did see it, especially when I would walk, when my mother would walk me, people would, we'd get the looks, and you know what I mean, like "Is that your kid?" "Is that really your mom?" So there was that element of it, but generally when we were in Lynn, we really didn't get it that much.

It was pretty standard stuff for African-American men back then to just feel disenfranchised, that they weren't getting their just due. My father told me at a young age that I was going to have to work twice as hard to get half of what someone else might get just based on who they were or who their parents were. My dad worked at GE for 30-something years. I mean he died working for GE, so he was, he definitely didn't sit back and take it. He was more of the type like I am, like I'm going to go and prove myself so anyone of any color wouldn't be able to deny me employment opportunity because I'm going to hustle so hard that it would just be ridiculous to deny me, and he had that same mentality.

Jason Taglieri's Brickyard

1

My reintroduction, my re-entry into the Brickyard area, was when I met Rocco. We were both doing music back then. He was about four or five years older than me and I met him through Fred Hogan. Fred Hogan used to DJ back then; he used to DJ at like a lot of the house parties out here and we were at a house party and he was DJing, me and my friends. He would put on instrumental music sometimes and invite people to come to the mic, sing, rap, whatever. So he did that and

Fred Hogan heard me and after the party he approached me and said, "I got a guy, a friend of mine named Rocco that you really should meet," so he gave him a call to set it up.

2

I came to the Brickyard to Rocco's parents' house and as soon as I walk up, I hear music blasting out of his windows, his bedroom windows like right in the front of the house. His window was open and that was kind of the cue to know that Rocco was there. If he was home, there was music coming out, so I walked up to the door and rang the bell. Rocco opened it and he kind of knew who I was and we went inside and the friendship kind of started from there—it was a mutual respect right away. We both had a lot of the same kind of musical sensibilities and just philosophically we were very alike. The way we looked at the work, so yeah, that was kind of the genesis of our friendship, and that was in probably 1989, 1990, so we've been friends for quite a while.

3

When we met, he was working with another artist, Sherwin, who I went to school with. He was more advanced 'cause he had been writing for a lot longer. So when I got there, Rocco was already involved in that project and we were kind of just developing something that maybe the two of us could do together. But then, eventually, we all kind of came together and formed one unit and I actually proposed that we call it Brickyard because there was another group out at the time, very popular, called Cypress Hill. They were on the West Coast and they were named for their neighborhood and so I said we should call ourselves The Brickyard.

So we joined forces. We were working on stuff all the time. I mean we gotta have at least ten or eleven complete songs as far as collaborations together go, and then we were always contributing to each other's projects. I would do an instrument on his; he'd do one on mine. We'd collaborate with writing so there was a lot, I mean there was definitely a lot of output in the late 80s to probably about the mid-90s.

4

The Brickyard was kind of a microcosmos of the whole city, so you had a diverse population. You had a lot of blue class, I mean blue-collar working-class people. Hard-working people. A lot of people who were second-generation Americans. Some first. There were a lot of Italians,

Just seeing that every day kind of definitely influenced our music. I mean Rocco's father to this day. If you drive down there on a Saturday, you will see him out there with a shovel or a chain saw. He's still actively maintaining his property. It's inspiring to me to see that kind of pride in the neighborhood. Definitely it bleeds over into our music.

MY MUSIC

I do hip-hop, so just beats, some rhymes, but I'm also heavily influenced by jazz. I listened to jazz since I was a baby. Motown, all the old classics were playing in my house, so I do a lot of instrumental stuff that's jazz inspired and actually, that's probably been the core of what I've been doing for the last I'd say ten or more years—instrumental jazz-based music.

Every year I record a little something just for my own collection, but it's definitely more producing and even over the years, just working with other younger artists and producing for them and just inspiring them and helping them with their creative process as far as writing and structuring songs and things like that.

It's been more about that than doing my own stuff. I'm never thinking, "I'm going to be a star. I'm gonna be famous." Music's just part of who I am. It's like breathing. So when people ask me, "Hey Jay, you still doin' music?" it's like, "You still see me breathing, right? Okay. So you don't have to ask that question."

CENTERBOARD

1

I started working for Centerboard, free-lancing, photographing events and doing some corporate head shots. Centerboard is basically a social service agency, and then I went to some of the homes in Lynn that they are in, and I did family photos for young moms and even the ones in transitional housing. With the advent of like digital photography and a camera in everyone's phone, no one has real family portraits anymore, you know what I mean, that are like official. I'd go into the homes and shoot these families, the moms and the kids, and print them out and give them an actually-physical item that they can have, an heirloom. That went over really big so I do that pretty much every year,

2

Some of the older kids that are in some of the programs that they run were heavily into music and wanted to write and sing, so when I saw that I said, "You know, how about we do a music workshop for the kids?" We had space for maybe 15, and that first time we got like 35 kids. I just expanded it and I said, "Alright, everyone can stay." The first class everyone introduced themselves, said what they did, and then how the classes were run, everyone would come in and just very quickly, we'd go around the room and figure out, "Okay, what's everyone working on this week?" And people would kind of tell each other and like just naturally, pairs would form up, groups would form up, so we'd have these natural pairings of artists get together and collaborate.

I'd walk around the room and if people had trouble just fitting words in or with the structure of songs, 'cause when you're young, you don't know all of that, how many bars are in a song or verse, a lot of it was just the science of crafting the song and then a lot of it was just helping them express what they had inside but didn't have words for. So doing that, it kind of opened up my eyes to the need for that kind of program, the need for that kind of guidance for these kids, 'cause otherwise they might go out and get into the wrong stuff. So that was kind of the bigger picture and at the end of the first workshop, we actually, we printed up about five hundred CDs. We did covers, we passed them out, we had a party, the parents came and the kids performed. It was awesome.

3

We did another one the next year, but it didn't attract as many people. A lot of the kids that had been in the transitional programs transitioned out of them, so we did do another one but it was a lot more casual. It was more like a place, a quiet place for them to create. It wasn't really geared toward a final product or a CD release. It was more like a quiet safe place where kids can create, do the things that they feel passionate about.

4

Centerboard wanted to take advantage of what they saw as the power of the huge upsurge in the arts and in their importance and visibility in the city. So that's when they approached me. They said they wanted to do a gallery, but they just didn't know how. They weren't versed in art at all, so they asked me if I'd be interested in helping them do that and I was like, "Yeah, of course." So you know we kind of talked about it for a couple of weeks, and then I actually brought Rocco in and I said, "Rocco these people are really serious about doing some art stuff. Would you be interested?" And he was like, "Yeah, of course." So we both came in and we actually did the first show for the gallery. I had photography up and Rocco had his paintings.

WHAT'S UP WITH ME

1

Right now I'm part of a group that's called the Brickyard Collaborative. It's basically a maker space, and they just recently acquired a nice-size location. The concept of a maker space, if you're not familiar, is you just have this space where people can just come in and they have like photograph equipment. They have a large format printer. They have power tools, they have metal working tools, they do cinema, so it's like basically a place where you pay a membership and you can come in and use the space any time you want and they have instructors and tutors to help you do whatever craft you want.

I'm working with them. They just had their grand opening about a month ago. They have a gallery space also, so I'm helping them curate their shows and kind of funneling the kids in the Centerboard programs over to them, depending on what they are interested in. If it could be beneficial for them to be there, and I'm pretty sure they're going to be having special programs for kids for free of charge, so that's a big part of it.

2

My end game? I would like to get a complex in the city kind of similar to a maker space, but geared more specifically towards photography, music and acting. I'd like to get those three disciplines in a building where kids can come in and have a safe environment to come learn, come practice and come get confidence. I'm all about kind of promoting alternative methods for success for kids who may not be traditionally looked at as potential success stories.

The crux of my life and my philosophy is to inspire people who don't have visible examples of success in front of them and prepare them to go out into the world with the tools they need to make it happen for themselves. With me, it's all about believing in yourself.

Fred Hogan

FRED HOGAN'S BRICKYARD

Growing up, the boundary of the Brickyard to us was always at the railroad tracks headed toward Alley St. Once you cross over the railroad tracks you were in the Brickyard. That's just how us kids always knew it. I'm from the other end of Shepard St., the end towards the Lynn Commons. Shepard St. goes all the way down to the Lynnway and usually, the other side of the tracks we would call the Brickyard. So Alley St., Harbor St., the other end of Blossom St., the other end of Shepard St., that whole area right there.

When I was a kid, my backyard was what became Marian Gardens. Lynn Housing came in and put up new developments. The empty lots became new families. Those empty fields became houses and they became new families so the neighborhood definitely changed.

We called it the Marian Gardens neighborhood. So Marian Gardens—we always had a place to go, we had friends over there. We had things like that just being on LaGrange Terrace.

I came to LaGrange Terrace in 1970, when I was six months old. I'm 48 now, so I've been here for 47 ½ years. Wow! You can say I'm a new school Brickyard person.

THE RAILROAD TRACKS

1

We used to go up the railroad tracks and we would, we had this weird thing that, we would put quarters and pennies on the railroad tracks so the train would come by and just squish them to make them big and that was a hobby of ours and it was a fun thing to turn a penny.

One afternoon, we were up there crushing coins. I don't know if the police came or something, but something sparked us to run off the railroads. We were running down the backside, the other side of the Brickyard behind Lynn Tech. We were climbing down the fence and the little thing, the latch that goes on the fence, one of our friends slipped into it and it went into his ribs.

He almost lost his life. The latch went right into him and back then, there were no cell phones. So we lay him on the ground, stuffed shirts in his wound and people, other friends, ran for help. We remember that as us going from crushing pennies and quarters to being at the ICU and praying for one of our good friends.

Back in the early 80s, they didn't protect the railroad tracks like they do now. They're fenced off really good and kids just can't get up there like they used to. We had easy access. We were walking the railroad tracks a lot. We hung out on the railroad tracks; we had forts up there behind the Brickyard. We would get doors from these old abandoned buildings and we'd build our little forts. We had blankets in there. We'd go over there and take naps and hang out and just do kids stuff. It was a great time for me, growing up in the Brickyard, just because we had friends from on that side of the tracks, from the other side of the tracks, and it was pretty cool.

OUR MUSIC

1

When I met Rocco Capano, he was another kid like myself. He got into trouble when he was a younger kid and then we both became DJs. We just loved music, we loved playing it, we loved making mixes, we loved doing all this stuff. So I would go over to Rocco's house and we would practice our DJing and stuff and his parents were old school Italians and they didn't understand. They didn't know if we were doing bad stuff or what, but as we talk to them nowadays, they are very excited that we were into the music and not into stuff that we could have been into.

So we spent many hours, many days at Rocco's house making mixes and practicing our music. We were DJs. We used records and Rocco used drum machines and stuff like that there, and he got into making the music like for rappers and stuff like that there, and you know for me, I was a seventeen-, a sixteen-year-old DJ and I was very popular in the neighborhood 'cause if someone had a party, they would have me do it so it was really fun.

2

Rocco's a special kid and I was lucky I linked up with him because we got to do positive things together and then we started doing gigs together. We started sharing our gigs and actually, he DJed my wedding 25 years ago.

That's the bond we have, and then an extra bond that I never knew would happen down the road is his big brother Pete Capano became the ward city councilor, and low and behold, right behind him is Fred Hogan and now I'm the ward's city councilor. But those two kids playing music in that room with Big Rocco, his dad not understanding what we were doing, and now you know we're positive role models in this neighborhood, so it's very special.

Instead of hanging out on Friday and Saturday night getting into trouble, I was the DJ. I was the DJ at all the parties, at the functions doing, I used to DJ Thursday, Friday and Saturday every week just 'cause I was so popular. We always used our own names. I was DJ Freddy H and Rocco was DJ Rocco C. We never had no weird name. We just did our regular old-neighborhood school-kid names. A lot of the 40-something-year-olds who are still in Lynn can always say that either at a middle school dance, or a high school dance, or a house party or anything, DJ Freddy H was their DJ. So it's pretty funny now. I will still walk into an event and they'll be like, "Hey! DJ Freddy H!" It's pretty funny stuff.

OUR GANG

You know what? Back then we didn't think we were a gang. We might have been a gang, but we called ourselves the LGT crew, which stood for LaGrange Terrace. That was our name for our basketball team. We were just friends. I guess we probably were like a gang, but we were more like just kids that grew up together that just protected one another and stuff like that there.

I'm the baby of eight kids who grew up in our house, so I had another gang too. I had my brothers and sisters. Nobody could mess with the Hogan gang because I was the youngest of the eight and if I ever had a problem, I had my brothers. Then each one of my brothers and sisters had their own group of friends, so if you put them all together, we had a pretty big group.

OUR HOUSE

1

Mind you we had this big giant house down there on LaGrange Terrace that you know was a great place. My mother would let all kinds of kids live there over the years that either had problems or whatever, because we always had an extra bedroom, and she would let, she would take kids in and help them out. When my mother passed away, she probably had twenty to thirty of those kids at her wake and funeral.

2

Well picture this here: you have a house with eight kids in it growing up and all their friends, and we had dogs over the years. We had this; we had that. My mother was a single parent. She raised us by herself. Our house got beat up pretty bad over the years, just wear and tear and things like that there, so my mother would do the little projects that she could do.

When I got married, I moved away, just not far away, and then I moved right back to Marian Gardens. I lived in Marian Gardens for nine years, like literally twenty steps from my mother's house. We started to help her do some projects around the house just to make the house a little better. My brothers did the basement over; they lived down there and had a nice apartment. We did the attic over; we had a studio apartment up there. And, this was a big four-bedroom house.

Then my mother got sick; she had a stroke. I was living at Marian Gardens, so I came back to take care of her, and before we moved in, we did a total remodel of the house. We put in a wheelchair ramp; we made the downstairs dining room a bedroom for my mother. I gutted the basement and redid the apartment so I could move my family in. I had four kids, so now it's I'm bringing my family into the house. So the house got a whole 'nother life.

3

I put a pool back in the backyard. When we grew up, we were the only family in the neighborhood with eight kids, so we had a swimming pool. My mother used to charge the kids 25 cents to swim in it, to pay for the chlorine. That was also a way to just keep the number of kids down. Just 25 cents back then was a lot of money, in the early 70s. When I moved back, the pool had been gone for probably fifteen, twenty years. I put the pool back in, and I put a deck in the backyard.

I put a deck on the front of the house. We did the siding over. We got a new furnace, a new roof. The house looks unbelievable. I'm prepared to live here a lot longer. So now I've watched my kids grow up and I've watched their kids grow up. It's pretty amazing that the house and the neighborhood have come through all these changes and now here it is—me and my wife. We're both under 50 and we're empty nesters already 'cause we started young. That's the little story about the house. The house probably saved my mother and it saved me over again and here I am now with four years left to pay on it.

OUR NEIGHBORS

1

When my mother wanted to call us, she had a good thing. She had the back deck. She could just yell to us. She'd yell "Freddy" and the whole neighborhood would echo "Freddy." That's how it was, how it was like even if I was three blocks away. We'd get the "Freddy" call from someone. There's no cell phone or anything like that. That's what a neighborhood really is. When my kids were growing up, my kids could go play in the neighborhood, and they'll be safe because it was just, that's how it was. So it's pretty cool.

2

Now you have to reach out to neighbors even more because people go to work, they come home, they get in their house, they don't really associate with their neighbors. I think that's the thing that changed—the association and the talking between neighbors. Not your neighbor right next to you, you might have that relationship, but what about two houses over? It's not like it used to be.

3

I'm a community guy. I have an organization called We are Ward 6. I'd like to build up community spirit. Like the Italian Club still does the bocce over there and Rocco Capano, he's almost 90 years old. He's still there playing. I go there one day, he wanted me to be his partner. He wasn't going on until 10:00 at night. I go, "I don't know about you, but I'm trying to get to sleep for work." Here he is ready to go his turn at 10:00 at night.

4

The Commercial St. end of the Alley St., it floods there too. So what is happening is on the Lynn Tech field, we are getting a pump station put in, which is going to help. Plus there is going to be new pipes put in the ground, so we're hoping that that alleviates a lot of the stress on the neighborhoods, because obviously me as a city councilor and working at the wastewater plant, I know exactly, directly, what's happening with the flooding, and I've been over there when people's houses are flooding.

My friend lost his boiler twice. It's a tough thing. It's a tough thing for a neighborhood, but that's another thing: when the flooding happens, you see neighbors coming together. One thing about Lynn is when something bad happens, everyone comes together for each other, whether it's the Brickyard, the Marian Gardens neighborhood, the Shepard St. neighborhood. East Lynn, West Lynn, it seems like everyone comes together for each other. Neighbors have each other's backs.

HOOPS

1

I started off coaching at Lynn Tech back in 1993 or something like that. I assisted there for nine years. We won a state championship—the first vocational school to win a public-school state championship, so that was pretty cool. Then after that, I had the head girls' basketball job at Lynn English. We turned the program from a 4-and-16 team into a perennial division champion.

Then I ran a basketball tournament in Lynn down at Marian Gardens for twenty years called the Hoganz Basketball Classic and then I got out about six years ago. I still do logistics for it, but now it's called The Shoe City Basketball Classic. We've got players and NBA players and college players that come from all over the place. We've got a thousand people out there watching in the summers. It's the biggest summer basketball tournament in New England.

2

It started with us. It started with four teams, the LGT crew, the Warren Street Raiders. We decided to have a neighborhood basketball tournament with four teams and then the following year four more teams got in. We had eight teams, we had Salem and then it just kept getting bigger and bigger and bigger and it peaked out at like 50 teams using multiple courts. Now it's about 32 teams, so it's amazing.

People come out at 9:00 in the morning for the first game with their lounge chairs and sit there all the way until 8:00 or 9:00 in the evening, and just in the last two years, we added lights so the games can go into the night. It's the best free basketball tournament in New England. People are having their little drinks in their lounge chairs and in 25, 26 years, not one incident happened down there.

The neighborhood has respected it, and with the gangs, we'd call a truce for that weekend and we would find out who was beefing and we try to talk to them prior to and say, "Hey listen. This thing's been going on for 26 years. We don't want to ruin it." We would reach out and we would get word, let's say this guy's beefing with this guy. We would call them and say, "Hey listen. We respect you. We respect you guys. We won't do anything here." And there's been a lot of respect for over 26 years. The community protects the tournament and we try to instill to them that as long as everyone's acting the right way down here, then it will keep going on.

Plus, the Marian Gardens basketball court has been done over. A friend of mine who owns a liquor store donated two basketball hoops—glass backboards with the collapsible rims. And we get the court done over every three years. It's probably one of the best maintained courts in the city and the kids and everyone takes pride in that. At Marian Gardens, we've brought bleachers in, and it's a stadium type atmosphere. There's a red carpet; there's VIP seating up front.

See when I did it, you had to win on Warren St. to get to Marian Gardens. You had to get out of that bad court and get to the good court. One time we had four NBA players and probably seven Division 1 basketball players playing over there on the cracked court and people are like, "What are you doing to these guys?" "Hey, they gotta win there to get over here." It was pretty amazing.

The tournament is the beginning of August every year, first weekend in August. It's the Shoe City Classic now. It was the Hoganz Classic. You can google YouTube Hoganz Classic and see some of the videos. It's unbelievable—some of the players that played in it.

Dave Waller

Dave Waller's Brickyard

I started a visual effects company in 1999, and my wife and I were trying to think of names for it. We came up with all kinds of crazy names, and we still have a little piece of paper with all the names. Then somebody told me, "Name it something that means something to you. Don't just name it like Happy Cat. You don't care about happy cats." So I thought about it and the Brickyard popped into my head because it was the neighborhood that my grandfather grew up in and told me a lot of stories about, and from all of his stories emerged a picture of a very special place and that meant a lot to me, that being part of my roots. I decided to call the company Brickyard VFX. To me, the Brickyard is an amalgamation of a lot of different ethnicities and ideas and people that all got together and made something kind of cool. That's what this company is to me.

It's always been a positive response to the name Brickyard. What I did learn quickly is that the name Brickyard is not unique to Lynn. Matter of fact, we tried to get brickyard.com and we found out it's the pit stop at the Indy 500. So every town, even Cambridge, had a brickyard. Any town of any size that had clay nearby. But our Brickyard that we talk about, there is something there that resonates about the honesty of the place and the inclusiveness of the place and that's something I think everybody would love to get back in their own lives.

I'm glad I live in this era, but I sure would wish that I could go back in time and experience those golden days firsthand. I really do think there's probably stuff we're missing, that we don't quite understand completely. We've got these little snippets and we're trying to composite an image of what it was, but I think when you talk to the people that have lived in the Brickyard, what emerges is this picture of a really interesting place that you'd really like to go and visit.

My Brickyard Grandfather

1

My grandfather's name was Jack Hines; he was the second oldest of five kids. His dad worked at the water gas plant and his, Jack's nickname, my grandfather's nickname, was Water Gas. And actually, my great grandfather, Michael Hines, he came from Ireland. He survived an explosion in the building there, which was a very dangerous thing. So what was your question?

Oh, that's right. So he lived on Shepard St. and he lived on Alley St. and I think he lived on another street too. They never had enough money to buy a house so they would always move around from one tenement to another. But pretty much that little corner there, they stuck within a block of that.

2

When he was thirteen, his mother, he heard her crying because she couldn't pay the rent that week, and he had saved some money that he had stashed in the basement stairwell in a little cavity. He went down and gave her the money for the rent and then he quit school and had to go work at the GE.

3

As a kid, he first just went around, he called it "picking links," which was taking dog excrement and selling it to the tanners up in Peabody, and when business was slow, he said that they would push some clay through a lead pipe for simulated dog poop and sell that, which the whole idea of faking dog poop to make money just seems like that's about as dirt poor as it gets.

He and his buddies would go underneath the telegraph wires along the Narrow Gauge waiting for the guys to drop pieces of copper wire down, and they would gather that and sell it to the rag and bone men that worked in the area. He made money drowning cats for five cents a cat. He would go around to people's houses that had a litter of kittens and put them in a bag and then take it down to the Saugus River and put a brick in the bag and throw it into the river. He would light fires for Jewish families on the Sabbath because they weren't allowed to strike a match. Do little chores like that for people. He was always scrapping around making a buck.

4

Then when he got a little older, he worked at the GE plant for a while, and then he started working at the ballroom in Nahant at a concession stand as a teenager and then he really took off. He and his best friend from the Brickyard, another guy named Jack, Jack Walsh, they started putting in driveways. They bought a model-T truck—a used one. This would have been about 1917, 1916, and the first day, they parked it too close to the trolley tracks downtown and the trolley swung around and the back end of the trolley lifted the truck off the ground and threw it against a building and wrecked it and it was a lot of money back then. He moved out of the Brickyard probably about the early 1920s, so all his stories are from that first couple decades.

My grandfather was never wealthy but always had money to put on the table and always helped people, and so I really took after him and listened to all of his advice and stories, and he became my main mentor in life about how to conduct myself, how to do business, how to work with people, how to work with difficult people. And so over the years, I collected recordings of him and I made a video for his 90th birthday party, which is that video there that I can show you a bit of, if you'd like to see it.

ARRIVALS

Once in a while there would be a ship coming in on the Cunard Line from Cork in Ireland. They'd read about it in the newspaper and since my grandfather was the second oldest, he was the oldest boy, he and his dad would take the Narrow Gauge down all the way to the ferry in East Boston, go across the harbor and they would find an Irish boy with a plaid tweed coat on and a suitcase that was just standing there on the pier. The family had saved money to get the boy to America and that's all they had.

Just a suitcase with no one to talk to and no papers or anything and so they would find one of those boys. They would bring him over to Jacob Wirth's or they would bring him to the Union Oyster House or they would bring him to Durgin Park and buy him a hot meal which is probably the first hot meal he's had since he left Ireland and they'd bring him home to the Brickyard.

They'd sleep in the same room as all the other boys. They'd get him a job at the GE plant or at the gas works. There was always so many manual labor jobs for Irish. And then the next time a Cunard ship would come, they'd kick him out and they'd go get another one. They figured they'd done their job and they put him on his way. So imagine over the years how many people went through. They just felt it was their obligation because they were Irish. They didn't know these people. It might have been that my great grandfather had been helped that way and he was paying it forward.

DEPARTURES

My grandfather said they used to haul the casket up with ropes because it was considered by the Irish unlucky to bring a body through a doorway. So when you had a wake, you would wake in your own home and so they would raise a casket up through. The guys would put ropes around it while the women were cooking. They'd bring in through a window. They would ice down the body because they couldn't pay for an embalmer.

They would mourn them for three days and three nights. During the day, the men would be working and the women would be cooking and grieving, and at night, the men would come home and everybody would get plastered and they would sing songs, and Irish wakes really did last three days, and then they'd take him out the window again, take him and bury him at, in this case, in St. Mary's cemetery, but my grandfather always said, "You know those dead guys looked better than the dead guys look today." The ice really worked.

NEON

1

When you like something, sometimes you don't even know why. You just do.

2

When I was nine, I was riding on my bike with my brother and we went in the woods and found an abandoned dump and I found a sign in the ground and I took it home and I thought it was kind of cool. There was another one there and I went back the next day and grabbed that one. All night I was worried that someone was going to steal the other sign, when in fact, it had been in the ground for a hundred years, so I don't think anybody was really going to steal it.

I really started getting going as a teenager and then after college, I got a pickup truck and then all hell broke loose. It was in the 70s and 80s, when they were cutting down old neon signs like old trees. No one wanted them. You wouldn't even have to pay for them or if you did, it was fifty dollars to take it away. And so I amassed my collection early.

Now they're becoming extremely scarce and they're getting valuable and they're a commodity and they're kind of all the things I don't really like. So it's very hard to find a really good neon sign anymore 'cause they're either not around or they're just precious, they're too expensive. But I really like the fact that I can restore them myself, fix them, fix the glass, fix the paint, fix the wiring and the sheet metal and bring some life back to them.

3

The thing that I like most is that each sign is a touchstone to a story. They're cool to look at as objects, but when you dig back into what was this business, you find so much more richness. About the auto parts store that was two Russian immigrant Jews that came over and were repairing carriages in Russia and learned how to repair cars and started a blacksmith. And you find photos of that business and the guys that started it and you realize it's all a part of the American Dream. So I don't collect Bud signs or Sunoco signs. I collect the one-of-a-kind signs that would be in neighborhoods.

4

Neon is kinetic light. It's light that moves. It comes in waves. A chain reaction. Lightning in a tube.

5

If you can draw something on paper, you can probably render it in neon, and so it's a really great way to express an idea very quickly, and when someone's in a car, you need to be able to make that impression in a second. Right? You can get creative with animating it and having it change color. There's so many little tricks over the years that people have learned to attract your eye. They only have a moment for you to say, "That is a place I want to investigate."

6

The sad thing is big businesses have come along and homogenized everything. There's no real uniqueness to the landscape anymore. It used to be signs were a great way to find your way because there'd be a big bunny like two stories high, this big bunny and you're describing where to go: "When you get to the big bunny, you take a right." Now there's a Dunkin Donuts there and you can't say take a right at the Dunkin Donuts 'cause there's another one on the next block.

Ted Dillard

TED DILLARD'S BRICKYARD

1

I had been wanting to do a maker space for quite a while, so we started working on that and in the meantime, we were driving around town and exploring Lynn a little bit and we drove underneath that underpass that has the Brickyard sign, which just struck me as completely strange. I had no idea what the Brickyard was. I mean out of nowhere there's this sign that says Brickyard. So I started doing some research and then I found Kathryn Grover's book and I read the book and started talking to people and learned more and more about it and I'm kind of into maps so I was really interested where the Brickyard was originally.

In the very early stages, I just needed a working name and since a maker space is by nature a collaborative, for some reason The Brickyard Collaborative came into my mind. I searched and the domain was available so I registered thebrickyardcollaborative.org and then the funny part was we had a big event. We started getting all this momentum going and I was talking to this small team that I had working with me at that point. I said, "Okay, we gotta come up with a real name now 'cause this, I just pulled this out of my hat," and all of them were like, "We love it. We like it. Why change it?" So, I was like, "Okay, fine. It's good. We got the domain. We're all set."

2

So that's basically how it happened. It was just a project name, but the funny part was, at one of these events, city councilor and now state rep Pete Capano came up to me and I knew who he was. I never really met him and he is very direct. He came up and said, "So what's up with the name?" and I knew very well that he lived in the Brickyard and he grew up in the Brickyard and I said:

> "Well, you know, here's the deal. It started off as just a name, but the fact is the Brickyard neighborhood in Lynn has been the center for industry and innovation since the 1600s. It is as it was— a blank slate. It was open land and gradually, as they were building in roadways and railways, it became a convenient place for stuff to happen, and so through the entire history of the city, the Brickyard has been where the economy starts and that's what we are doing.

Manufacturing has changed in the 21st century, technology has changed, everything has changed, but what's happening in maker spaces across the country, in fact across the world, is you're getting people starting up micromanufacturing. Starting up, trying out new ideas, setting up little businesses, starting local economies. And so I'm not at all uncomfortable with using the Brickyard name for what we are doing and the side joke is that we rent out space to members to use as studios and they're ten by ten feet square so they're the same size as the shacks that they used to make shoes in."

So Pete, you know, he's not a man of a lot of words and he just kind of nodded his head and said, "OK," and he's been a staunch supporter of us from the beginning. He understands what we are trying to do.

3

I feel like the right way of putting it is that the Brickyard Collaborative is in harmony with the Brickyard spirit. We have our own animation and energy and there's a lot of stuff going on here. I would say most of our members probably don't know much about the Brickyard, but they come in 'cause they want to learn the laser cutter; they want to learn the traditional letterpress, which comes from the 17- and 1800s. They want to learn current and 21st century micromanufacturing techniques and this is the same thing that drove some guy to start making shoes in a ten-footer. It's just like, "I can do this. I gotta learn how to do this," and so that's the spirit that we have here. That's what I would say we are in harmony with, and I'm not gonna claim that the energy comes from the Brickyard.

4

If I make any money on this project, it will be because I'm going to write a book called, *I Started a Maker Space on Facebook*. I promote the maker space practically 90%, maybe 95% through Facebook. There are a couple of pages: "What to Do in Lynn" and "You Know You're from Lynn if You…". And so I joined those, and occasionally, if we have an event, I'll post it on there.

When we opened our doors, we had a big open house and I posted it. And then you get people posting: "I grew up in the Brickyard," "My mother grew up in the Brickyard," "We still live in the Brickyard." So completely off topic from what I was trying to do, but I just found it fascinating. It's like it's still a neighborhood that people identify with, which I just think is wonderful.

THE BRICKYARD COLLABORATIVE

1

The idea behind a maker space is that it's sort of a health club for tools. You have all these tools available, all these processes, all these things and you pay a monthly membership fee and you get access to all that and you get a discount on classes to learn how to use it. So you want to learn how to use a 3-D printer? You take a little class. You learn how to use a 3-D printer and then you can come in 24/7 whenever you want to and make 3-D prints. Same thing for the electronic and robotics lab.

I got a kid who comes in and edits photos on the photo station over here. We have a letterpress studio, we have a laser cutter, we have a C&C router, we have milling machines, we have a full wood shop. So you know for $75 a month you get access to any of that.

2

And what you also get is a lot of incidental use of something. For example, this is going a little bit deep, but I had a project where I had to mount three linear bearings. I had to drill four holes on either end of this piece of plywood perfectly aligned so the bearings wouldn't bind. I tried to do it for the last seven or eight years and I've never been able to. I've used my every means and I've been working in a wood shop my entire life. I could not get this thing accurate enough and we have a C&C router. It's about $2,000–3,000. We got it for the maker space and I'm scratching my head and all of a sudden I go, "Well, I could do this on the C&C router and it would be perfect." And I did. I drew it up, threw it on the router, did a test and it was absolutely perfect. I would not go out and spend $3000 for a C&C router to drill eight holes, but I have access to that now.

3

The second thing is collaboration. My very short story is about a young woman from Lynn who got all excited about the laser cutter and she starts laser cutting everything. Then she starts laser cutting ceramic tile. She's going to Home Depot and buying ceramic tile and she's engraving the ceramic tile and then she rubs a little ink in there from a magic marker or something and it looks awesome.

So, then we have this other member who's very good friends with her and he rebuilds teletype machines from 1965, which are all running on punch code tape, and so he has all these illustrations and art things that he's made with punch code tape. Well then suddenly he realizes he can engrave punch code tape onto ceramic tile because of what his friend is doing and he is putting out this really amazing looking work based on his little take on what she does with that technology.

4

There's another story about a maker space in California where these kids were out of college and they had been working on an incubator for premature babies. They were trying to use a plastic, a polymer to produce heat to keep the babies warm, 'cause if they're two weeks premature, they have a very short period of time to live if they don't get into an incubator to maintain their body temperature.

So they're standing around talking, and this guy walks by and he says, "What are you doing?" They tell him about the project and he says, "How much do you know about polymers?" "We know nothing about polymers. We just got out of school." You know, it turns out this guy has been working with polymers for thirty years and he multiplies their heat yield on this polymer ten times. So basically, he donated his core technology, their core technology, over a cup of coffee in this maker space and the result is they've saved 85,000 babies' lives since they developed this product. That's something that's not insignificant.

5

And there's a guy in the Artisan's Asylum, a maker space in Somerville, and he's developed a little device, and he started a Kickstarter program for it and raised 3.1 million dollars, and that's money that comes from the world and comes into Somerville, and what we are trying to do here is to get money coming in from the world into Lynn, where it's always come you know, because of manufacturing.

IT TAKES A VILLAGE

My 25-year-old son said to me the other day, "Look, you've been doing this for 1½, 2 years, and look what you've done." I had somebody the other day a while back actually say that I did this through my own force of will. That couldn't be further from the truth.

The Brickyard Collaborative was embraced by the community immediately. There were people that just dove in, and some of them didn't even really know what a maker space was. Some of them have gone off to other projects and we've brought in other people, and it's like it's a changing community, but we have a friend, in Ireland actually, who's been very supportive of what we are doing. Our sister city in Ireland, which Mayor Tom McGee connected us with, the mayor there sent a video congratulating us when we opened and he said, "You know they say it takes a village to raise a child. Well it certainly takes a village to start a maker space," and that's absolutely the truth. Now we have like something like thirty people involved, who are members, who are board members, and are all doing what they can to make our maker space a success.

Ralph Tufo

RALPH TUFO'S BRICKYARD

From what I've read, the Brickyard ended on one end at Commercial St. We lived four blocks over on South St., actually South St. Court. So officially, although I wasn't in the Brickyard, I was very close. I had a lot of interaction in the Brickyard due to the fact that my mother grew up there, her family and all her cousins. And we would visit them.

My major involvement with the Brickyard was St. Francis Church. We were all members. It was sort of an Italian community church and I remember my brother and I, on Sunday we would walk through the Brickyard and go to church and then afterwards, we'd go to the Jewish bakery and get ourselves a treat.

One of the things that was sad about the demolition that occurred in the Brickyard is that a lot of people, including my relatives, moved out. And as a result, the number of parishioners at St. Francis diminished. We kept going even though we didn't live in the Brickyard and, over time, eventually the church closed and that was a very sad thing 'cause it was the center of our Italian community in Lynn.

RECREATION

1

For recreation we would go to the junkyard on Bennett St. and throw rocks at the rats. That was our big thing. We were very much into rock throwing.

There was a train that came from Bennett St. and went in back of South St. and ended up going to the General Electric, and there were these coal bins right on the railroad tracks right in back of my house pretty much, and for a recreation, friends and I used to go in the coal bins and roll around and get covered in coal dust. My parents were not too happy about that.

2

Then every day at 3:00, no matter where we were in our neighborhood, 'cause we didn't really go out of our neighborhood much, we were usually playing baseball in somebody's backyard or King of the Hill or something like that. We would stop whatever we were doing, gather around the edge of the railroad tracks with our rocks, and try to pummel the train as it came by. Now some of my friends got a little more adventurous. It was not a fast-moving train, but they would put like different things like logs or rocks or whatever on the train tracks so that they'd have to stop, and when they stopped, we had a better chance of pummeling the train because it wasn't moving.

3

We would have rock fights with groups from different parts of the city, like Shepard St., which was very close to where we were. I don't know how anybody coordinated that, but it was all a game. It was not even you know, like we were like fighting over something. It's just what we did and it all seemed like a game until my best friend got hit in the head with a rock, and he started bleeding, and I said, "Oh my God! This is for real," and so, then after that, I didn't get involved in any more rock fights.

FIRE

1

My mothers' side of the family was definitely in the Brickyard. My fathers' side of the family is from Revere. My father was a fireman and a lot of my mother's cousins were also firemen. Vassalos, my uncle, was the Chief. His brother Carmen was a fireman in Lynn.

They were all in Lynn and my uncle Vinny Petrola was also a fireman and all of them died young, including my father, from fighting all the fires in Lynn. Arson was rampant. There were a lot of fires and back then, the fireman didn't have the protective gear that we have now, and so my father died at 54, and all of my uncles died young too.

2

I wrote this song called "The Brickyard Blues," which is about arson in Lynn. I based it on an actual rooming house fire that occurred in 1989. It wasn't in the Brickyard, but very close, and what happened is that the landlord shut the second exit out of the rooming house, nailed it shut and didn't maintain the smoke detectors. Four people died and the landlord was brought up on involuntary manslaughter charges. The paper said they believed there was arson, but they couldn't prove who was the arsonist.

So I took that story, and I wrote this song called "The Brickyard Blues," from the point of view of a person who was in the rooming house, who was staying in the rooming house. It's about how he survived and how the owners of buildings make a profit and how there's only ashes and stone left and a burnt-out lot and burnt-out land. The song goes, "Arson for profit. It's a dangerous game."

3

This song "The Brickyard Blues" is part of the play that I'm working on right now called "Beyond the Blues," which is set in the Brickyard in 1982 at the Urban Legend Bar and Grill. It was saved from demolition by this group led by the owner of the club, who was able to save this portion of land. He renovated this bar and grill and hosts blues-music open mics, and so this play is about an open mic blues competition that takes place in the Brickyard close enough to the time when the demolition occurred so people still have fresh memories and can remember how they were affected by that.

4

My cousin told me this story and I refer to it in "Brickyard Blues' and I don't know if it's 100%. I can't validate for this to being true, but he told me this, he's ten years older than me, that his friend's father who lived in the Brickyard, he organized a demonstration of the neighbors in the Brickyard who were opposed to the demolition and he said they marched on City Hall, some of them with shotguns. They marched, and he also said that his friend's father pulled a shotgun out on the guy who was surveying his land, you know, ready for demolition. So I don't really know. I can't vouch for this actually being true, but this is the story that was told to me.

THE ACCORDION

1

I started taking lessons when I was five. My grandfather on my mother's side, all my relatives, all my grandparents were from Italy, he played the accordion, so it was kind of in the family. My older brother had taken lessons and stopped. My cousin Selena who was older than me had taken lessons as well and she was really really good.

So it was in the family and we used to watch "The Lawrence Welk Show" as a family and I remember from what my mother said is that while we were watching, I started like pretending I was playing the accordion on my stomach, and so she said, "Oh, get this boy accordion lessons." So I took accordion lessons and then whenever we had these family get-togethers, they would make me drag my accordion out to play for them. I had to play "Oh Marie" 'cause my older cousin who was my babysitter was Marie, and I had to play all these other Italian accordion songs, which I really didn't want to do, but I felt like I had to.

2

We have a picture of me with a gigantic accordion; I think I must have been like six years old. Yeah, I played pretty much until I got to junior high school and then it was not cool to be playing the accordion so I kind of taught myself how to play the piano, just learning the left hand. Then I really just played piano, until after graduate school, I got roped into playing at a party for Irish music, which I had not played ever. And then I was playing the accordion with the Gloucester Hornpipe and Clog Society, and I ended up being in that band for about thirteen or fourteen years, playing jigs, reels, British Isles hornpipe music, international folk music. So accordion playing came back to me.

3

Myron Floren was the featured accordion player on "The Lawrence Welk Show." Lawrence played the accordion, but most of the time he was conducting the band. Myron Floren was a virtuoso and would play polkas, gypsy music and South American music. All different kinds of music on the accordion. And one time Myron Floren came to Lynn to give a concert. It might have been at the Lynn Auditorium, I'm not absolutely sure, but my parents, my mother mostly, tried to make arrangements for me to play for Myron Floren, either before his concert or after, some kind of gathering, and basically I didn't do it. I didn't want to. I don't know what it was. I didn't want to be embarrassed? I just decided I didn't want to do it. It could have launched my national career as an accordion player.

4

Lawrence Welk was something that we all looked forward to: my mother, my father, my two brothers. We all gathered around and watched it. It wasn't like it was corny or anything back then. I remember there just being a nice feeling.

URBAN RENEWAL: POCKETS OF POVERTY

There were pockets of poverty in different parts of the Brickyard, but not the entire Brickyard. I remember some of the tenements around Commercial St., when I would walk from South St. to St. Francis Church, some of the tenements that were closer to Commercial St., I guess what is now Neptune Towers, yeah, there was definite poverty, but other parts not really, parts sort of in back of the railroad tracks.

From what I can gather, it was kind of a shame that everything got knocked down because like I say, it put our church out of business. It wasn't the entire area and honestly, there was as much poverty in the Highlands as there was in the Brickyard, so I mean they could have knocked down places in the Highlands if they were looking for pockets of poverty.

When I go through there now, I see empty spaces, empty lots. I see the high-rise buildings of Neptune Towers and I ask, "Is this better?" I don't know. Why is it we don't restore things? We knock things down. "Did it have to be the way it turned out?" I don't know the answer and that will always remain a question in my mind.

More About
the Brickyard

FROM URBAN RENEWAL TO
NEIGHBORHOOD DEVELOPMENT

1

Urban renewal might not have killed the expanded Brickyard by itself, but in the end, it was a stake in its heart. The Brickyard was a neighborhood that could not survive the demolition of the majority of its area and the rebuilding of that area with, most visibly, affordable housing towers and a vocational high school. Tenement housing fostered personal relationships among neighbors and being carless tied those neighbors to each other and the neighborhood. Brickyarders displaced by urban renewal lost not only their homes, with many feeling inadequately compensated, but also an entire network of social relations. Plus, shortcomings in the governmental administration of urban renewal in Lynn added fuel to a firestorm of grievances that still smolders to this day.

2

Placing the urban renewal of the Brickyard within the big picture of post-World War II America begins with the passage of the Housing Act of 1949, which signaled the start of federal funding for modernizing American cities via urban renewal. That money lasted until 1974, when the government replaced its urban renewal programs with Community Development Block Grants.

There were some spectacular humanistic failures of urban clearance and renewal in the decades preceding its arrival in the Brickyard. Perhaps the most famous of these is the demolition of the East Tremont neighborhood in the early 1950s in order to construct the Cross Bronx Expressway in New York City. The losses suffered by the displaced were dear, and when Robert Moses, the director of the project and many others like it, was asked by his biographer Robert Caro to reflect on their plight, his oblique answer gave Caro the impression Moses wasn't really concerned about people. Caro also reports in his recent memoir *Working* [2019] that, to expedite their leaving their homes, East Tremont residents were sent completely false notices of eviction in ninety days. And finally, and perhaps most egregiously, the entire neighborhood could have been spared had the expressway been moved just two blocks. Moses decided not to do that for his own political ends. He did not put people first.

Closer to Lynn was the urban renewal of Boston's West End, a process begun in 1958 and lasting into the early 60s. In his book, *Building a New Boston* [1993], renown Boston historian Thomas H. O'Connor quotes Lawrence Kennedy: "The West End symbolized all that was wrong with city planning in the 1950s because it bulldozed the homes of poor people and replaced them with an enclave for the wealthy." O'Connor himself concludes, "The City's first major redevelopment effort produced such a violent public reaction that it jeopardized the whole future of urban renewal in Boston." Sociologist Herbert Gans, in his 1982 revision of *The Urban Villagers* [1962], outlined twenty ways to improve urban renewal based on his analysis and evaluation of what went wrong in the West End. But by then, it was too late. The damage was done. In the West End, there was one tenement left standing—the Last Tenement—one narrow three-window wide four-story building that has become iconic.

Historian Kathryn Grover's excellent treatment of urban renewal in the Brickyard begins with Lynn Mayor Thomas Costin's intention, announced in 1956, to utilize federal funds to underwrite an urban renewal project that would alter the Brickyard forever. Grover and Gans agree. More care should have been taken to assess the livability of individual houses before knocking a whole area down, and this belief seems common among displaced Brickyarders. By 1963, after a few bumpy years, Brickyard urban renewal was "up and running," as Grover writes. In 1964, the Lynn City Council approved the Lynnway-Summer Project, which included most of the Brickyard, and in 1966, the Lynn Redevelopment Authority began taking Brickyard properties by eminent domain. By 1967, the seizure and demolition were well underway, and by the mid-1970s, most of the area's redevelopment had occurred.

3

The misgivings and grievances of displaced Brickyarders are voiced in Grover's book, and a number of other irregularities regarding the Lynnway-Summer Project are addressed in the *Review of Certain Aspects of the Urban Renewal Program in Lynn, Massachusetts*, a report (B-118754) submitted in 1973 by the Comptroller General of the United States on behalf of the Department of Housing and Urban Development (HUD). In all, fifteen charges against the Lynn Redevelopment Authority were investigated, and the conclusions confirm some of the sources of anger among Brickyarders.

There were irregularities and delays in payments to displaced homeowners and they were not clearly told they could dispute the amount the LRA initially "awarded" them for their properties. Some people allowed to remain in their seized properties were charged rent even though they had yet to receive payment for those properties. There were many legitimate complaints about the shortcomings of the relocation process. And significantly, the report noted community participation in the Lynnway-Summer Project in the manner prescribed by HUD was absent from 1971 to 1973.

The report refers to one community group without naming it, Citizens for a Better Lynn, and mentions its opposition to the Lynnway-Summer Project since early 1968. The group advocated for more housing rehabilitation and complained about a lack of housing for the displaced. In July 1972, Antonio Marino, the former president of CBL, was elected mayor, and also that year, CBL members who had become elected officials were among those who brought the charges against the LRA that prompted the Comptroller General's report.

Incidentally, the report stated that in April 1973, the Lynnway-Summer Project was 70% complete and would be done, the LRA estimated, in March 1976. Through March 1973, Lynn had spent 17.9 million dollars on urban renewal, including the much smaller Market St. Project, which began in 1962. The U. S. Department of Housing and Urban Development paid 10.6 million dollars of that total, or about 60% of all expenditures.

Concurrent with urban renewal in the Brickyard was the War on Poverty. Begun by President Lyndon Johnson in 1964, it was overseen in the Brickyard by Lynn Economic Opportunity Inc. (LEO), the local community action agency of the federal program. The Brickyard Neighborhood Council was a community organization that was part of this anti-poverty effort. The BNC was started by the Rev. Paul V. Donovan of St. Mary's Church, and it had a working but contentious relationship with LEO, at least until Rev. Donovan was transferred to Roxbury in the fall of 1969.

Rev. Donovan is an unsung Brickyard hero. He's not mentioned by either Grover or Gecoya and yet his impact on the neighborhood in the 1960s was huge. Rev. Donovan came to St. Mary's in 1958 and stayed eleven years. *The Lynn Item* article of October 19, 1969, "Testimonial Planned for Father Donovan," observes that because Father Donovan believed "the church must identify itself with the problems of an area through action, he formed Marian Gardens, a non-profit corporation whose purpose was to sponsor medium income housing in the urban renewal area under Federal Housing Bill 221-D3. The work of the corporation is now evident in the Summer Street Renewal Area, where 94 units of housing are nearing completion." Two distinctions matter here. Although part of Lynn's urban renewal in general, Marian Gardens was not developed by the LRA, which brought housing towers to the Brickyard. In contrast, Marian Gardens consisted of two-story garden apartments.

Furthermore, as president of the BNC, Father Donovan led it to develop pioneering programming for pre-school children. What began as a summer project grew into Project Head Start, and the article states, "Father Donovan brought the program into existence one year before it became a federal activity." Surely, for bringing Marian Gardens and Head Start into the Brickyard, Father Donovan deserves to be remembered, and certainly, for creating human-scale affordable housing, he deserves credit for implementing a progressive step forward in urban renewal both in the Brickyard and in Lynn.

In addition to the Lynn Vocational Technical Institute, a public high school that opened its new campus in 1971, urban renewal brought 900 new affordable apartments to the Brickyard, all of them north of the B&M/Commuter Rail tracks. These housing projects were intended to replace the aging housing destroyed by urban renewal. Even though they may not have replaced all of the lost housing units, to be fair, they did go a long way toward fulfilling that promise of urban renewal. However, all of the buildings on the following list except Marian Gardens stack their apartments vertically in a larger-than-human scale. Only the two-story Marian Gardens spreads its apartments out horizontally on a human scale.

Wall Towers   2 towers   9 floors   176 1br apts.   senior/disabled housing
  Tremont St.   1967

Marian Gardens   14 two-story buildings   94 apts.   44 2 br   43 3br   6 3br
  open housing   Blossom St.   1968 (renovated 1999)

Neptune Towers   2 towers   12 floors   334 apts.   142 1br   144 2br   48 3br
  open housing   Neptune Blvd.   1971

YMCA   four-story building   68 bedroom units   open housing   Wheeler St.
  1972

Connery Skating Rink   Harbor & Shepard Sts.   1972

St. Stephen's Tower   1 tower   10 floors   130 apts.   senior housing   Bond St.
  1976

St. Mary's Plaza   seven-story building   99 apts.   senior housing   Pleasant St.
  1981

On the list above, the outlier is the Connery Skating Rink. Obviously not housing, it was built as part of the Lynnway-Summer Project on the site of the Connery Playground in the original Brickyard south of the B&M/Commuter Rail tracks. It was the only building constructed by that project below the tracks. In *Remembrances*, Chick Gecoya quotes a letter to *The Lynn Sunday Post* from a fellow Brickyarder which refers to the playground as "the heartbeat of the Brickyard," "almost like a second mother." The writer calls the rink "a tombstone to the memory of our playground." These days, hardly anyone coming to the rink for hockey or skating remembers much about the Connery Playground.

6

East Tremont, the West End, the Brickyard. By demolishing the physical neighborhood, destroying the network of social relations that creates a sense of community, and then failing to provide an adequate amount of compensatory housing, a whole way of life can be erased.

It wasn't just the politics of housing that led to the demise of these neighborhoods. The rise of the automobile after World War II required that urban renewal entail road building as well. East Tremont made way for the Cross-Bronx Expressway, Boston's Central Artery, opened in 1959, preceded the transformation of the West End, and in 1955, the Lynnway opened. These roadways were built to accommodate the automobile, something most people who lived in self-sufficient walking neighborhoods didn't need and probably couldn't afford.

In addition to the impact of the automobile, stressors on the Brickyard included an outmigration to the suburbs by Brickyarders who were able to leave, the general deterioration of an aging housing stock, a long-term downturn in the local economy once driven by GE and the ever-declining shoe industry, and a higher proportion of renters, who by definition, do not have a stake in maintaining property. The demise of the Brickyard neighborhood as it existed in the decades after World War II was inevitable, and as difficult as it was for those displaced, now, fifty years later, it may be more fruitful to look at urban renewal, not as a death knell, but as a phase in the life of the Brickyard. It was a steppingstone to the concept of neighborhood development, which seems like, and even sounds like, a more sensible and humane way of achieving the same goals.

7

In Lynn, neighborhood development, seen as a better way to revitalize the city, took the form of Neighborhood Development Associates. Established in 1979, this non-profit housing agency is overseen by a board of directors and its administrative responsibilities are managed by Lynn Housing Authority & Neighborhood Development (LHAND). The website of NDA <www.ndainc.org> states its goal of working with the city of Lynn, LHAND and the citizens of Lynn to reclaim and build property in order to create stable healthy neighborhoods where residents take pride in their homes.

Brickyard Village, an NDA project opened in 2005 on Warren St. and Shepard St., between Summer St. and the Common, shows what urban renewal has become in the 21st century. Interestingly, Brickyard Village is located in the only area in the Brickyard Corridor above the tracks not impacted by the Lynnway-Summer Project. Brickyard Village has three distinct and varied parts to it, 28 apartments in all. One part is five connected two-story townhouses, the second is five houses, eight apartments, in close proximity, and the third is a cul-de-sac cut in from Shepard St., June Lane, expressly created for its fifteen units in nine garden apartment buildings. The closed-offedness of the cul-de-sac, along with the human scale of the buildings and their ample yard space seem designed to foster community. And could there be a better name, a better brand than Brickyard Village? And how about its tag line: "A Roof Under the Stars."

The NDA brochure for Brickyard Village describes each of the three facets of Brickyard Village as lavishly as a realtor might. The three descriptions end identically. The townhouses have porches that "create a neighborhood feeling and a sense of home." The five houses offer landscaping "to create a feeling of relaxation and home." The cul-de-sac on June Lane is "a safe and pleasant place to call home."

In 2005, Brickyard Village won a prestigious Doorknocker Award from HUD in the category of Neighborhood Development. The official citation lauded Brickyard Village for, among other things, beautifying and improving the infrastructure of the neighborhood, adding parking, even repairing the exteriors of existing houses. Brickyard Village's "architectural designs blend with the surrounding neighborhood and do not look like low-income housing." Indeed, Brickyard Village reflects very well on NDA as it shows what urban renewal looks like in the 21st century.

In brief, the Brickyard illustrates the history of urban renewal in America during the 75 years since World War II. The examples in this essay show that first in the Bronx and then in the West End, and finally in the Brickyard, urban renewal demolished neighborhoods, displaced people, and disrupted social relations and communities of many kinds. In the Brickyard, affordable housing in towers and garden apartments replaced torn-down tenements. Only a small portion of the neighborhood remains intact. Memories preserve the old neighborhood more than anything else.

Neighborhood development has superseded urban renewal. Brickyarders would probably agree that what the Brickyard needed wasn't urban renewal but neighborhood development. Rehabilitation and building. Human scale housing. Community participation. Interagency cooperation. All things NDA. The history and evolution of urban renewal in the Brickyard begins with the Lynnway-Summer Project of the 1960s and culminates in 2005 with Brickyard Village. Lesson learned. From urban renewal to neighborhood development, it's all there in the Brickyard.

THE LITERATURE OF THE BRICKYARD

1

The literature of the Brickyard is fascinating, extensive and impressive. The most important Brickyard writer is Vincent Ferrini (1913–2007). Vincent was born in Saugus, grew up in the Brickyard and always identified with the neighborhood. The classic poetry collection *No Smoke* [1941] was based on Ferrini's Depression-era experiences with the people and the city of Lynn. "Julia Brennan" profiles a well-known Brickyard resident and "The City," "The Factories," and "The Narrow Gauge" critically capture their influence on life in the neighborhood in the 1930s.

Ferrini's subsequent books, *Injunction* [1943], *Blood of the Tenement* [1945], *Tidal Waves: Poems of the Great Strikes* [1946], *The Plow in the Ruins* [1946] and *Onions and Bread* [a lost 1936 manuscript rediscovered in 1998] solidified his reputation as a working-class poet and preceded his 1948 move to Gloucester, where, with Charles Olson, he became one of the city's epic poets, famed for his multi-volume *Know Fish* [1979–1986]. And even though Ferrini had been living in Gloucester for forty years when it was published, *Hermit of the Clouds: The Autobiography of Vincent Ferrini* [1988] revisited his upbringing in the Brickyard and described how it contributed to the formation of his identity as a poet.

2

In the wake of urban renewal, *The Lynn Item* published a series of Guy "Chick" Gecoya's reminiscences of the neighborhood as he knew it. These were later collected in an unpublished manuscript, *The Brickyard Story: Remembrances of Times Past* [1979]. When reading *Remembrances*, what's immediately noticeable is the recitation of names. So many Brickyard names are mentioned, it seems Gecoya (1916–2001) knows everybody. This reflects the custom of many Brickyarders, who'll easily rattle off the names of their neighbors and friends on their street. Gecoya establishes himself as the "unofficial historian" of the Brickyard by the sheer volume of the information he provides about individual Brickyarders and their families.

The tone of Gecoya's writing shows he's proud of their accomplishments. The many boxers spotlighted illustrate one way the American Dream was pursued in the Brickyard, and all the mentions of success in junior high and high school sports show the scope of Gecoya's knowledge of neighborhood achievements. For Brickyarders, a goal in life was to become "prominent," and Gecoya's *Remembrances* celebrates many Brickyarders who rose to prominence in their chosen fields.

However, and this is not surprising when you think about it, Gecoya's is a mostly male-centric depiction of the Brickyard as he knows it, and his proposals that the first use of the Brickyard name occurs just prior to 1900 and that "real" Brickyarders only come from the four-block area he grew up in, put him and his generation at the center of the neighborhood's story as he tells it.

And in the immediate aftermath of urban renewal, when it was time for those who "survived' it to gather again, at the first and second Brickyard Reunions held in 1973 and 1974, Chick Gecoya was a prime organizer and the emcee who proclaimed inclusively, "We are Brickyarders all." And if there is a poem that represents the nostalgic and idealistic spirit of these reunions, it is "The Brickyard: Remembrances of Times Past…" by Brickyard poet and educator Anthony Cama. It appears in the program for the second Brickyard Reunion and also as the foreword to Gecoya's manuscript. The last verse of the poem reads in part, "Somewhere, some place, where heaven's angels play… Brickyard heaven waits for you and me."

3

Six other Brickyard authors and a group of Lynn high school students are also noteworthy.

John Frasca (1916–1979) was Brickyard born and a journalist in Tampa, Florida, when he won a Pulitzer Prize in 1966 for local investigative reporting. The story of his role in freeing a wrongly convicted Black man is told in *The Mulberry Tree* [1968]. Despite not having lived in the area for many years, Frasca's name is frequently mentioned when the achievements of Brickyarders are inventoried.

Vito Adamo Jr. wrote "The History of St. Francis of Assisi Church," a concise and comprehensive essay included in the booklet accompanying the celebration of the Fiftieth Anniversary of St. Francis Church in 1975.

In 1980, North Shore Community College Upward Bound students produced *Voices of a Generation: Growing up in Lynn during the decline of the Shoe Industry,* a booklet of oral histories. In it, the Brickyard is prominently featured. In addition to some Brickyard stories, photographs of the original Brickyard are included, as are the art and voices of Arnold Trachtman and Vincent Ferrini.

Nathan Gass (1908–1992) was a Brickyarder whose recollection of arriving in Lynn from Russia is included in *Brickyard Stories*. He founded the North Shore Jewish Historical Society and his article, "Jews found home in Lynn," was published in *The Lynn Item* on April 14, 1976. Gass includes information on the Brickyard's synagogues and the Lynn Hebrew School, and he mentions "that in 1908, the Lynn Jewish Social Branch no. 2 of the Socialist Party held meetings every Friday evening at 19 Blossom St." A pamphlet, "The Jews in Lynn: A Retrospective" revised this article and was first printed in 1987.

Gass' goal of creating a history of Lynn's Jews may have helped motivate Alan S. Pierce (1948–   ) to put together *The Jewish Community of the North Shore* [2003], a potpourri of photographs and captions in the Images of America series that features many scenes of Jewish life in the Brickyard. Pierce's *A History of Boston's Jewish North Shore* [2009] includes an update of Gass's 1987 pamphlet, a scholarly treatment of Jewish participation in Lynn's shoe industry by Stephen Mostov and photographs of Lynn's Jewish community.

Short Stories of a Long Journey: An Oral History of Russian Jewish Settlement North of Boston [2002] by Bernice Kazis (1924–   ) is a product of her work as Director of Russian Resettlement for the Jewish Family Service of the North Shore. This book nicely complements the section in

Brickyard Stories 2.0 about Neptune Towers and helps place those stories in a wider historical context.

Finally, the autobiography *From the Chicken House to the Court House* [2004] by Bruce N. Sachar (1933–2019) vividly describes growing up on Shepard St. and working in the family business, Singer's Poultry on Blossom St.

Although the Brickyard has a strong presence in Sachar's book, Adamo's essay and in the Upward Bound booklet, less of one in Kazis's book and in the work of Gass and his successor Alan Pierce, and none in Frasca's, the publications of all of these writers can and should be considered part of the literature of the Brickyard.

4

There's even a literature of urban renewal in the Brickyard. Jim Steadman's "The Brickyard— A Changed Neighborhood," published in *The Lynn Item,* describes the state of the renewal on October 2, 1972. Wall Towers, Neptune Towers and the vocational high school are built, and the Y and the Connery Rink will be done soon. Steadman's article includes that tidbit about the 1880s origin of the Brickyard name as well as people's criticisms and comments about urban renewal.

The essential document however is the *Review of Certain Aspects of the Urban Renewal Program in Lynn, Massachusetts*, a report submitted in 1973 to the House of Representatives Committee on Banking and Currency by the Comptroller General of the United States on behalf of the Department of Housing and Urban Development. The report (B-118754) is available online and it clearly details the shortfalls of urban renewal in the Brickyard. Together, the article and the report provide a snapshot of a time when much of the work of urban renewal has been completed, but there is still more to do.

5

In addition to *The Lynn Item*'s March 21, 1969 article, "Darrell O'Connor Creates Lynn 'Land of Oz,' " two other newspaper articles merit inclusion in the literature of the Brickyard. "Roots Deep in Ethnicity, Lynn Sustains Melting Pot Tradition" by Kathy McCabe appeared in *The Boston Globe* on May 5, 1991. McCabe does a terrific job of reviewing the history of immigration in Lynn up through 1990, and she portrays the Brickyard as a quintessential immigrant neighborhood. She includes quotes from Walter Boverini, the pastor of the Bethlehem Temple Pentecostal Church, and Gladys Haywood, "the unofficial historian of the city's black community." A photograph of Haywood and her daughter Delores Jackson in front of the Lynn Public Library is at the article's head.

The unsigned article, " 'The Brickyard' was a great place to grow up," was published in *The Lynn Item* on November 17, 1998. This article focuses on the Brickyard before urban renewal and recounts Chick Gecoya's story of how the Brickyard got its name. And although a map of the real

Brickyard according to Gecoya is part of the article, it does state that the Connery Family was "arguably the first family of the area." This creates a seeming paradox. How could it be that the real Brickyard is below the B&M Railroad tracks while the first family's coal business at Connery's Corner is above the tracks at the corner of Wheeler and Pleasant Streets?

6

Last are two approaches to writing about the Brickyard taken by academically oriented authors. My *Brickyard Stories: A Neighborhood and its Traditions* [1985] is a fusion of oral history and poetry in the service of storytelling. In an introduction, to give readers a background for the stories they are about to read, I sketch a history of the Brickyard and its growth and assess the neighborhood's importance to the people who lived there and to the city.

Kathryn Grover's *The Brickyard: The Life, Death and the Legend of an Urban Neighborhood* [2004] is a treatment of the neighborhood by a trained historian hired by the Lynn Museum and supported by the Eastern Bank and Massachusetts Humanities, the state's branch of the National Endowment for the Humanities. Grover's history is comprehensive—there are many helpful statistics, and it includes Chick Gecoya's detailed hand-drawn map of the "real" Brickyard done expressly for the book. Grover's clear historical presentation of urban renewal in the Brickyard provides valuable context for the many stories Brickyarders tell about it. And Grover places Barchy DeNino at the center of the legendary Brickyard. When I did my interviews in 1982, it was clear his scrap metal business, located next to the Italian American Citizens Club, was a social hub, and it was also apparent that for many people, Barchy and the Brickyard were synonymous. I'm glad Barchy got his due in Grover's history because I regret mentioning him only peripherally in *Brickyard Stories*.

7

Brickyard Stories 2.0: A Lynn Neighborhood Before and After Urban Renewal picks up where Grover left off, revisits the neighborhood, and posits a reply to the question raised by the title of her book, "What happens to the Brickyard when the legend withers?" The short answer is that the neighborhood shrinks and the name becomes a brand.

Brickyard Stories 2.0 offers longer stories that sometimes intersect and together seek to create a rich tapestry of neighborhood life. My accompanying essays propose there is a literature of the Brickyard and that the neighborhood is a crucible in which urban renewal evolved into neighborhood development. I've included a cache of maps to envision the history and development of the neighborhood as well as photographs of the Brickyard Corridor in 2020. I've done my best to enable you to become a Brickyarder too.

BRICKYARD 2020

1

Today, the Brickyard that represents the robust expanded Brickyard in its heyday is a shrunken neighborhood and an expanding brand. Today, the heart of the Brickyard is located between the Commuter Rail tracks and the Lynnway, essentially on Harbor and Alley Streets. Today's Brickyard abuts Chick Gecoya's real Brickyard and is about the same size. Gecoya's real Brickyard ran from Blossom St. east on Harbor and Alley Streets over to Pleasant St.; today's real Brickyard goes west from Blossom St., encompassing all of what's left of Harbor St. as well as the residential part of Alley St., which ends half-way between Shepard St. and Commercial St.

2

In today's Brickyard, both ends of Alley St. are given over to business and industry. Between the Commercial St. end of Alley St. and the Lynnway, auto shops have taken the place of Lynn Lumber, which was in business there from 1945 until 2013. On Alley St. between Blossom St. and Pleasant St., commercial development is also dense with transportation-oriented enterprises, including a diverse range of car repair garages: Caruso's, Pudgy's, Caribbean, E & M, Italmondo, Spina's and Global. On the other side of Pleasant St., across from where one end of Harbor St. once was, the Lynn Storage building still stands. Opened in 1908 as the biggest building in America exclusively dedicated to storage, it still serves the same purpose, though now it's called Life Storage.

3

Today, the "Brickyard" signs under the tracks on both sides of the Commuter Rail bridge on Blossom St. keep the neighborhood's name alive. In today's Brickyard, there are four places that have direct historic ties to the Brickyard in its heyday. DiFillipo's Brickyard Bar and Grill on Blossom St. is owned and operated by Rocco DiFillipo, son of Armand DiFillipo, who owned and operated The 50 Club in the same building. The 50 Club followed in the footsteps of the legendary Lennon's bar, which is associated with Chick Gecoya's story of how the Brickyard got its name. The Italian American Citizens Club on Harbor St. was founded in 1935 and Barchy DeNino's father was one of the eight original members. Today, the club's activities inside its brick building and outside on its well-groomed bocce courts keep Italian Brickyard traditions going.

Next to the Italian Club, on the corner of Blossom St. and Harbor St. is the building Barchy DeNino used to conduct his scrap metal business and to stable his horses. Still there today is a small stone memorial to one of Barchy's horses, Jackie Daniels, who died in 1985 at the age of 16. Finally, also on Harbor St., but facing Shepard St., the Connery Skating Rink honors the great Brickyard Irish political family. Installed in 1972, the commemorative plaque inside the building reads: "The Connery Memorial Rink   Dedicated by the MDC in memory of the late Wm. P.

Connery Sr., mayor of Lynn 1911–1912 and his sons the late Wm. P. Connery Jr., Congressman 1923–1937 and the late Lawrence J. Connery, Congressman 1937–1941."

4

Today, the area cleared by urban renewal has a completely different look, feel and purpose to it. The land north of the Commuter Rail tracks and south of Summer St. and Neptune Blvd., from Commercial St. to Blossom St., is occupied by Neptune Towers, the Lynn Vocational Technical Institute, its athletic fields and the Neptune Boulevard Playground. Between Blossom and Pleasant Streets, north of the tracks and below Neptune Blvd. and Tremont St. (formerly Summer St. here), what was J.B. Blood's food market is now KIPP Academy Lynn Collegiate, a charter high school. The nearby YMCA is expanding dramatically. A large new building under construction will focus on adult fitness when complete and will enable the old building, dating from urban renewal, to be used entirely for youth development. Nearby, the former St. Francis Church is now a center for children, home to the Blossom St. Head Start Center and the LEO Head Start Day Care.

And in the area bounded by the YMCA, KIPP Collegiate, Neptune Blvd./Tremont St. and Pleasant St., Eliot Community Human Services occupies a sprawling one-story building with ample parking. The mission statement on its website reads: "Eliot is committed to serving the most vulnerable of populations—those at risk, with limited or no resources for help." Finally, in the far southeast corner of this area, where Pleasant St. goes under the Commuter Rail tracks, tall on the brick wall rising behind the restaurant Jamaica's Flavor: the mural portrait (my favorite) "Sipros Big Ears."

5

Summer St. is no longer a mecca for shoppers. Today, there's only a handful of businesses. The RK Dollar Discount store, the Amigo Market and El Tikal—Taqueria & Pupuseria (Guatemalan) are located at the west end of Summer St. near Commercial St. Two Dominican restaurants, Tipico and the shuttered La Ruta, are just beyond the east end of Summer St., on the north side of Neptune Blvd. near Blossom St. The Washington STEM School lies behind them. Opened in 1916 as the Washington School, it's the largest visible throwback above the Commuter Rail tracks to the heyday of the Brickyard. And now it has a contemporary focus.

Marian Gardens is across from the school between Blossom St. and Shepard St. Off Shepard St., one block north of Summer St. toward Lynn Common, is June Lane, Brickyard Village's cul-de-sac. West of Shepard St. one block north and parallel to Summer St., Warren St. is home to two beautiful blue and gray full length basketball courts used in The Shoe City Basketball Classic, the annual summer hoops tournament whose championship is won on the short court at Marian Gardens.

Finally, at the eastern end of the Brickyard Corridor above the tracks, north of where Neptune Blvd. becomes Tremont St., between Pleasant St. and Church St., the two Wall Towers and the modern home of the Lynn Housing Authority and Neighborhood Development nestled between them create a housing plaza complete with courtyard. St. Stephen's Tower stands adjacent to the Wall Towers and St. Mary's Plaza is on the other side of Pleasant St.

6

Today, over fifty years after the Lynnway-Summer Project began, between the Commuter Rail tracks and Lynn Common, on land that was once part of the expanded Brickyard, you'll find schools (Lynn Tech, KIPP Collegiate, Washington STEM), affordable housing (Neptune Towers, Wall Towers, St. Stephen's Tower, St. Mary's Plaza, Marian Gardens, Brickyard Village), and community and social services (the Eliot, the YMCA, Blossom St. and LEO Head Starts, The Shoe City Basketball Classic). All these institutions make essential and vital contributions to the well-being of area residents.

That said, it's hard to consider the area north of the Commuter Rail tracks as part of the 21st century Brickyard below the tracks. Brickyard Village may be as close as it comes. It's the Brickyard name, perhaps used nostalgically, an excellent name for the location. Maybe it evokes the best ideals of the old Brickyard and maybe it reflects the altruistic motives of Neighborhood Development Associates. Nonetheless, in this case, the Brickyard name is more of a brand than anything else.

To Brickyard Village add Brickyard VFX, DiFillipo's Brickyard Bar & Grill, The Brickyard Collaborative, The Brickyard hip-hop collaborative, the performer called The Brickyard Prince, even the Brickyard signs on the Blossom St. rail overpass.

Now there it is—the Brickyard in 2020—still alive—a shrunken neighborhood and an expanding brand.

A September 8th 2020
Photo Safari
Through the
Brickyard
Corridor

Photographs by Rod Kessler

Photographing the Brickyard

1

In the summer of 1984, North Shore Community College ran a two-week program for Lynn high school students designed to interest them in attending the college when its new permanent campus opened. I was co-leader of "Lynn Words/Lynn Pictures," and when it was time for the students go out into the city to take Polaroid snapshots, my colleague Beverly Verrengia organized what she called a "photo safari," a phrase that has stuck with me.

2

On September 8, 2020, I took writer and photographer Rod Kessler on a photo safari through the Brickyard Corridor, the area between Commercial St. and Pleasant St., running from the Lynnway up to just south of Lynn Common. We started in the original Brickyard, and as we worked our way down Alley St. to Pleasant St., Rod snapped shots of the old Brickyard from back in the day. Then we visited the portion of the corridor north of the MBTA Commuter Rail tracks, and there, Rod photographed the new, post-urban renewal Brickyard.

One of the stops on our safari was the basketball court at Marian Gardens, where the summer basketball tournament started by Fred Hogan is held. There, quite by accident, we met Ernie Pleasant, the long-time Marian Gardens groundskeeper who has been honored for his service by having the small park that surrounds the court named for him. Ernie was a little suspicious of us at first, and wondered what we were doing there, but after chatting, he said he was happy to make our acquaintance. As we walked away, I told Rod I felt it had been a magical encounter and that Ernie probably could tell us some great Brickyard stories.

To finish up our safari, we headed back into the original Brickyard, passing underneath the Blossom St. Commuter Rail overpass with the Brickyard signs on both sides of it. We were going to Harbor St., the heart of the new "real" Brickyard as I call it. In particular, I was looking for a memorial Barchy DeNino put up for one of his "hosses". Rocco Capano told me there is a stone plaque in memory of Tony on the back wall of his former place of business, which faces the bocce courts at the Italian American Citizens Club. It wasn't there, so I asked inside at the Club and was kindly directed to its actual location. Finding it felt like a mystery solved and a quest fulfilled. It was the perfect end to our photo safari and that put us in a great mood as we made our way to DiFillipo's Brickyard Bar & Grill for an outdoor lunch.

The photographs taken by Rod Kessler on the September 8, 2020 photo safari show the Brickyard Corridor in the present day. For those interested in what the Brickyard looked like in the past, photographs of the neighborhood before urban renewal can be found in a number of books, most prominently, of course, Kathryn Grover's *The Brickyard: The Life, Death, and Legend of an Urban Neighborhood* [2004]. Grover's *The Lynn Album II: A Pictorial History* [1996], also contains photos of the Brickyard, including one of Rev. Paul V. Donovan speaking with a Summer Circle resident about her upcoming relocation due to urban renewal. Joanne S. Foley's *Lynn* [1995], part of the Images of America series, shows J.B. Blood's in 1910, as well as the original St. Francis Church and the first St. George Greek Orthodox Church. Both the firehouse on Commercial St. and Huntt's Dairy Lunch in Central Square are in Diane Shephard's *Lynn Massachusetts* [1998], part of The Postcards of America series. And among the many photographs in Frank Kyper's *Narrow Gauge: A Nostalgic Window on the Boston, Revere Beach & Lynn Railroad* [2010] is one of the West Lynn station on Commercial St.

The photographs in *Brickyard Stories 2.0* portray both the new "real" Brickyard, between the Lynnway and the MBTA Commuter Rail tracks, where the legacy of the Brickyard before urban renewal is most visible, and the post-urban renewal Brickyard Corridor above the tracks. Between the tracks and the Common, a lot has changed in the fifty years since urban renewal began, and it's important to recognize and celebrate the fruits of that process. These photographs show where Rod and I went on our photo safari through the Brickyard Corridor one sunny morning in the late summer of 2020. They contain echoes of the past, but more importantly, the pulse of the present and the promise of the future.

The New "Real" Brickyard Below the Tracks

The Brickyard sign on the Neptune Blvd. side of the Blossom St. Commuter Rail overpass is seen while heading south toward the Lynnway into the new "real" Brickyard. It was either this sign or the one (below) on the other side of the overpass that inspired Ted Dillard to name his maker space The Brickyard Collaborative. Read "Ted Dillard's Brickyard," pgs. 244-245.

The Brickyard sign on the Alley St. side of the Blossom St. Commuter Rail bridge has been damaged. Looking north through the overpass the spire of St. Mary's Church is visible. Read Ruth Tansey "St. Mary's," pgs. 153-154.

This house at 140 Alley St. was once the home of James McNiff and his family. Read "James McNiff's Brickyard" and "Why We Moved Out of The Brickyard in 1942," pgs. 93-94.

Here is a close-up view of the home-made memorial in front of 140 Alley St.

Walter Boverini was born in 1924 on the second story of this building at the corner of Alley St. and Blossom St. In the 1980s, after urban renewal, Gordon Laro met his Brickyard pals on Sundays at the corner store on the street level. Read Walter Boverini "Urban Renewal," part 4, pg.77, and Gordon Laro "Brickyard Corner Stores," pgs. 165-167.

DiFillipo's Brickyard Bar and Grill on Blossom St. occupies the same building that The 50 Club did after it was relocated there following urban renewal. Read Armand DiFillipo "The Fifty Club," pgs. 69-71.

This is the cement balustrade fence on Alley St. that James McNiff remembered being constructed in the 1920s. Read James McNiff "No Cracks," pgs. 94-95.

Many members of the O'Connor family worked at this Pleasant St. facility when it was named C. Bain. Opened in 1908, it was then the largest building in the US used exclusively for storage. Read Judy Christian and Chris Maniatis "C. Bain," pg. 113.

The Italian American Citizens Club on Harbor St. was founded in 1935.

The Italian American Citizens Club features two well-maintained bocce courts. Read Fred Hogan "Our Neighbors," part 3, pg. 236.

The Connery Rink on Shepard St. is named for three members of the Connery family, Brickyard Irish who were very successful in politics. A plaque in their honor is in the rink's lobby.

JACKIE DANIELS
DIED 1985
AGE 16 YEARS

Barchy DeNino's stone monument memorializing his "hoss" Jackie Daniels sits near the building on Blossom St. that housed his scrap metal business.

The Brickyard Corridor Above the Tracks

The Wall Towers opened in 1967 and are located between Church St. and Pleasant St. This was the first housing development completed by the Lynnway-Summer Urban Renewal Project.

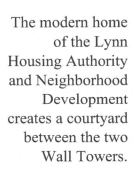

The modern home of the Lynn Housing Authority and Neighborhood Development creates a courtyard between the two Wall Towers.

St. Stephen's Tower opened in 1976 at the corner of Bond and Pleasant Streets.

The Washington School, now the Washington STEM school, opened in 1916 on Blossom St. near Neptune Blvd. Read Paul Benson "Culture Shock," pgs. 172-173.

Tipico Restaurant serves Dominican food and is located on Neptune Blvd., near the east end of Summer St. The Washington STEM School is behind it and a sign for the shuttered La Ruta restaurant is to the right.

A few stores anchor the west end of Summer St., near Commercial St.

The basketball court at Marian Gardens is where the finals of the Shoe City Basketball Tournament are held in August. The spire of St. Mary's appears in the distance underneath the backboard of the near basket. Read Fred Hogan "Hoops," pgs. 237-238.

His surname painted on diagonally opposite corners of the court at Marian Gardens represents Brickyard city councilor Fred Hogan's founding of the Hoganz Classic (now Shoe City) summer basketball tournament. Walking in the background at the far end of the court is long-time Marian Gardens groundskeeper Ernie Pleasant.

The cul-de-sac on June Lane, off Shepard St., is part of Brickyard Village, an award-winning housing project created by Neighborhood Development Associates that opened in 2005. Read "From Urban Renewal to Neighborhood Development," section 7, pg. 261.

The June Lane cul-de-sac creates a safe and charming place to live for both kids and adults.

The basketball courts on Warren St., used in the Shoe City summer tournament, are in good repair, beautifully painted and inviting.

Rockmere Gardens, located at the northern end of Commercial St., was built in 1900.

The twin Neptune Towers on Neptune Blvd. contain 334 apartments and opened in 1971. The twelve-story towers dominate the landscape and offer affordable housing to renters of all ages. Read stories told by residents of Neptune Towers on pgs. 198-215.

Also in 1971 on Neptune Blvd., Lynn Technical Vocational Institute opened its new campus next to Neptune Towers. Pictured here is the central concourse.

At the hub of the Brickyard Corridor above the tracks, a wide and leafy thoroughfare is created at the intersection of Neptune Blvd. and Blossom St. The east end of Summer St. branches off from Neptune Blvd. half a block west of this corner.

This building on Blossom St., which was home to St. Francis Church, now houses childcare facilities. The church's original building, once a mattress factory, burned down in 1954. The church began offering mass in its new building in 1956. Read "Ralph Tufo's Brickyard," pg. 248.

A new YMCA building is being constructed next to the old building on Wheeler St., which opened in 1972. Between the two buildings, the former St. Francis Church is in the foreground, and far behind it are the Neptune Towers.

This building on Wheeler St., once the location of J.B. Blood's market, is now used by the KIPP Academy Lynn Collegiate, a charter high school. Read Ruth Tansey "J.B. Blood's," pg. 153.

The fabulous mural "Spiros Big Ears" is at the corner of Wheeler and Pleasant Streets, near the Commuter Rail overpass.

Seen from Alley St., in the distance, are signs of the 21st century—wind turbine blades and a billboard for a marijuana dispensary.

Carl Carlsen stands in a Lynn Tech parking lot looking through the Shepard St. Commuter Rail overpass into what was the original Brickyard and what is now the new "real" Brickyard.

ACKNOWLEDGEMENTS

First off, a tip of my hat to the late John Fox, Professor Emeritus of History at Salem State University, who got me started in the field of oral history and mentored me in the early going.

As regards my work on *Brickyard Stories 2.0*, all writers need community, and I found mine at the meetings of the Salem Writer's Group, where six of these Brickyard stories were workshopped. I also received valuable feedback and support from writers Rob Wilstein, J.D. Scrimgeour, Ralph Tufo, Phil Primack, and Rod Kessler, who was kind enough to take the book's photographs. M.P. Carver did an amazing job turning my manuscript into a book. Sue Walker at the Lynn Museum was very helpful with some small stuff that made a difference. Daily, my wife Susan and our daughter Lindsey enabled me to do my best. Last but not least, my sincere gratitude to all the storytellers I've interviewed over the years. They are the book.

ABOUT THE AUTHOR

I taught English at North Shore Community College from 1974 through 2011. While there, I published *Brickyard Stories: A Neighborhood and its Traditions,* compiled *The Poetry of Lynn: An Anthology with Talking Points*, and wrote *The Soul of the City and its Vessel: Lynn Poetry in the Nineteenth Century.* For community service, I organized and emceed public programs showcasing local poetry with the Gloucester Lyceum, the Nahant Historical Society and, most notably, with the Lynn Museum, a decade-long annual Celebration of the Poetry of Lynn held in April, National Poetry Month. That all led to my creating the website *The Poetry of Places in Essex County:* <www.poetryofplaces.org>.

In retirement, I have written an oral history of my father's career as a master mariner, *Fifty Years on Seven Seas: A Life Aboard "The Ship,"* available on the Norwegian War Sailor Registry website: <https://www.krigsseilerregisteret.no/en/sjofolk/415616/default>. I also prepared a collection of stories from my mother's family, *They Came Out: Holocaust Diaspora Testimonies of the Lange Family,* available on the United States Holocaust Memorial Museum website: <https://collections.ushmm.org/search/catalog/bib267550>.

Brickyard Stories 2.0 completes what I've long felt to be my unfinished Brickyard business.

ABOUT THE PHOTOGRAPHER

I'm the son of an artist who was always trying to get my brothers and me to really *see* when we looked. I picked up a camera seriously in my twenties and once had my own darkroom, mixed the developer and fixer. I remember the smells. Sometimes I miss the heavy cameras with all the dials and the lenses, not to mention the tripod. These shots were taken on a cell phone.